P

How To Write Your Blockbuster

Fiona McIntosh is an internationally bestselling author of novels for adults and children. She is a travel columnist and co-founded an award-winning travel magazine with her husband, which they ran for fifteen years before Fiona became a full-time author. Fiona roams the world researching and drawing inspiration for her novels. Although South Australia is now home, she admits her best writing is done from the peace of Tasmania.

Her first attempt at writing a novel was made in the year 2000 after attending the Bryce Courtenay summer fiction writing school. The manuscript was purchased immediately by a major publisher and since then Fiona has released two books per year; she promised Bryce just prior to his death that she would continue his legacy of helping new and emerging writers on their journeys into commercial fiction through her masterclass.

fionamcintosh.com
fionamcintosh.com/masterclass

TESTIMONIALS FROM THE FIONA McINTOSH COMMERCIAL FICTION MASTERCLASS

'To my enormous delight, Fiona McIntosh will continue to run a Masterclass Writing Course. I can think of no writer who would do so with more professional aptitude and sheer pizzazz! Go for it, writers. It will change your life!'

BRYCE COURTENAY, SEPTEMBER 2012

'Without a doubt the Masterclass is a valuable opportunity. Fiona delivers a total package – a writing course that not only gives you hands-on experience and access to a wide range of writing strategies and tools but also empowers you to believe in yourself as a writer. If you're committed to becoming the best writer of commercial fiction you can be – this is the class for you.'

TRICIA STRINGER, AUTHOR OF *RIVERBOAT POINT*

'*Yes—we'd like to publish your book.* The seven best words I've ever read. And it probably wouldn't have happened if I hadn't participated in Fiona McIntosh's Commercial Fiction Masterclass. After five days with Fiona, and a room full of other inspiring writers, I came away knowing commercial fiction was what I write, and what I want to write . . . I feel the life I was made for has finally begun in earnest.'

MEREDITH APPLEYARD, AUTHOR OF *THE COUNTRY PRACTICE*

'I truly believe I wouldn't have sold to a major New York publisher but for Masterclass . . . [Fiona] unlocked my mainstream creativity and gave me permission to write my book, my way, without apology . . . It was a career move well worth making.'

LISA CHAPLIN, AUTHOR OF *THE TIDE WATCHERS*

'Without reservation or hesitation I can honestly say that Fiona McIntosh and Masterclass got me published ... Now, as I sit in front of my computer with a book deal with HarperCollins and a career as a writer, I am so thankful I made the right choice.'

SUSAN GALLINA, AUTHOR OF *THEY DO, I DON'T*

'Fiona transformed me from a flip-flopping procrastinating over-planner into a gun-slinging organised professional. She didn't just give me tips on how to make my writing better, and some amazing contacts in the industry (although that was all in there), but she changed the way I write forever. I honestly feel the Masterclass is one of the best things I've ever done for my writing, and I cannot recommend it highly enough. It will blow your mind.'

ADAM CECE, AUTHOR OF *WESLEY BOOTH SUPER SLEUTH*

'I had been struggling to write a novel for over four years ... Then I attended Fiona's inaugural Commercial Fiction Masterclass and I can honestly say I have never looked back. From day one, Fiona's love was tough, but I swallowed my pride and spent the rest of the Masterclass really listening and putting into practice her teachings.'

LISA JOY DAVIS, AUTHOR OF *YES, CHEF*

'The course will inspire, motivate and give you opportunities that you won't get anywhere else, and the cherry on top is you get to know Fiona!'

SAMANTHA NAPIER, AUTHOR OF *DATING THE ALPHABET*

'Fiona McIntosh's Masterclass helped me to understand with glaring clarity precisely what was getting between me and a publishing deal.'

DIANNE MAGUIRE, AUTHOR OF *WHAT MATTERS MOST*

'A captivating saga of love, loss, and the triumph of the human spirit . . . Fiona McIntosh is an extraordinary storyteller.'
BOOK'D OUT

'A perfect blend of romance, action, mystery and intrigue by one of our best known and popular authors.'
NOOSA TODAY

The Tailor's Girl

'Sure to appeal to lovers of period romantic dramas like *Downton Abbey*.'
WOMAN'S DAY

'Written with zest and a talent for description that draws you into the world of the novel and its characters. Fiona McIntosh is a prolific and superior writer in the genre, and if you enjoy popular romantic fiction, you'd be mad not to try her.'
THE AGE

'Everything I want in a curl-up-on-the-sofa read . . . *The Tailor's Girl* is an exquisite story that just bursts from the pages and leaps into your heart.'
WRITE NOTE REVIEWS

Nightingale

'Dreamily romantic and historically fascinating, this is McIntosh at her best.'
BRISBANE NEWS

'A book for readers who enjoy a fairytale romance.'
BOOKS+PUBLISHING

FIONA MCINTOSH

How To Write Your BLOCKBUSTER

A practical resource for the aspiring novelist

All I've learned about writing commercial fiction

PENGUIN BOOKS

PENGUIN BOOKS

UK | USA | Canada | Ireland | Australia
India | New Zealand | South Africa | China

Penguin Books is part of the Penguin Random House group of companies
whose addresses can be found at global.penguinrandomhouse.com.

Penguin
Random House
Australia

First published by Penguin Group (Australia), 2015

Design by Laura Thomas © Penguin Group (Australia)
Front cover image of book by CoraMax/Shutterstock.com;
back cover image of pencil and glasses by PlusONE/Shutterstock.com
and paper by Winston Link/Shutterstock.com
Author photograph by Anne Stropin at Chesser Studios
Typeset in Adobe Garamond Premier Pro by Laura Thomas
Colour separation by Splitting Image Colour Studio, Clayton, Victoria
Printed and bound in Australia by Griffin Press, an accredited ISO AS/NZS 14001
Environmental Management Systems printer.

National Library of Australia
Cataloguing-in-Publication data:

McIntosh, Fiona, 1960- author.
How to write your blockbuster/Fiona McIntosh.
9780143572381 (paperback)
Fiction—Authorship/Fiction–Technique./Creative writing.

808.3

penguin.com.au

MIX
Paper from
responsible sources
FSC
www.fsc.org   FSC® C009448

For Mum and Dad.

Apparently, aged five, I earnestly announced that I would be a writer one day and they believed me. Gosh! That's all anyone ever needs, for someone to believe in them – the rest is easy.

CONTENTS

INTRODUCTION

To write is a verb. At school I was taught that a verb is 'an action word'.

So, no more procrastination. Today's the day you get active and begin the journey of writing your novel.

People find their way to writing for all manner of reasons. Some of us are scribblers from a young age; others take to it in later years. Because it sounds sort of cool, I wish I could say that I had to write or I couldn't breathe. But that would be a whopping lie. Writing was an option for me. I could have taken up other pursuits but I chose to create stories. My writing career was spawned by nothing more banal than the midlife crisis of turning forty. At this oddly emotional milestone some people buy a fast car, some people go trekking in the Himalayas, and a few have extreme makeovers, get divorced or have affairs. My response to the fear of becoming lost to middle age was to attempt to write a novel.

Sad, isn't it?

It doesn't even sound remotely exciting. And yet if you were standing in my shoes at the time, you'd know that nothing could have been more daring, more dangerous, more thrilling than to be balanced on the precipice of life, staring into the abyss of my fifth decade, and actually doing something to shut up those whispering demons that were telling me I was too old, that I would fail. It would have been so easy to let the yearning go and allow the demons to win. After all, they were simply cautioning me that I was chasing an empty dream: reminding me that I was a mother, a wife, a business owner with responsibilities and that pursuing this notion was not only hollow but also downright selfish.

Plus, everyone wants to write a book, don't they? There are so many aspiring writers out there. Most believe they have a book in them. What made me think I could craft a story? I'd never played with poetry or short stories. I hadn't written anything creative since my school days, and I'm not especially cerebral or inquisitive. I don't gossip, I pay little attention to topical events and I don't read celebrity magazines. Worse, I'm not even that interested in people so I'm not a natural people watcher, and the human condition doesn't intrigue me nearly as much as animals do. I believed I had few of the traditional traits that show themselves in novelists. What was I thinking?

Did I really imagine I could stand alongside all those top sellers?

Bizarrely, I did.

Yes, it was selfish but still I chose to chase that dream. I want to reassure you, dear aspiring writer, that it did not cost me my family, my friends or my sanity. And I am now living the dream as a full-time writer who earns her living from novels. I'm still married to the same fellow, still cooking and cleaning up after our sons, still running a demanding, albeit different, business but feeling a hell of a lot more in control of my own destiny. And, above all, I am happy. I love my life, I love what I do, and I love to write.

Let me emphasise that writing wasn't a long-held dream. I didn't grow up with any burning desire to craft a novel. I did possess a voracious appetite for reading though and if experience tells me anything, it's that from the great horde of readers – the ones who dare not leave the house without a book kept close – come so many of the writers of the world.

I realise now that my self-revelation to write a book came when I was thirty-six years old but at that time it was a quiet notion; it took three years to fester and take shape before I found the courage to say aloud to my family and friends, 'I'm serious about writing a book'. That decision happened at thirty-nine when I was feeling anxious about that forty milestone. Rather than seek enlightenment in the Himalayas or have my face filled with botox, writing a book was the pathway that beckoned, then demanded

I walk down it. Before I knew it I was booking a flight to
Hobart to take a fiction-writing course with the amazing
motivator, and one of Australia's most beloved novelists,
Bryce Courtenay.

That's when my whole focus changed.

I'd spent years playing a support role to my children and
to my husband in his work, and now, at last, I was going
to be entirely selfish for a week. What I didn't take into
consideration was that I would experience the epiphany
that Bryce warned might happen. Over the course of the
week, as the concept of being a writer slotted firmly into
place, I knew that I was going home to discuss selling our
business and that I was going to shape the rest of my working life around creating commercial fiction. It seemed that
I needed that week away from all things familiar – away
from the confines of home and work rigours, from the
routine and structure of my life – to accept what had obviously been nagging away at the depths of my subconscious
for years.

I wanted to be a writer.

I went home from my week in Hobart, I sat down at
our kitchen table each night and I wrote like fury. I had
a finished manuscript in twelve weeks because I was
disciplined.

The discipline trait came naturally. I'd always had a
strong work ethic and I'm inherently ambitious. Plus I'd
been running a small, flourishing travel magazine business
with my husband for the previous dozen years so I knew

about seeing a job to its close, no matter what the obstacles were. At the time we also had twin nine-year-olds to care for, along with dogs to walk, family to visit and a whole other life that took precedence over my late-night story-telling. I used to sit down at my computer at 10 p.m. once the children were asleep, Ian and I had shared a cuppa and he was reading in bed, and the household was silent. I'd usually write for three hours. It wasn't hard, especially since I'd given up television (there was no social media then but there were plenty of distractions that I shut out). I learned to live on a few hours' sleep plus I scaled back our social life: not that we were party animals, but if an invitation got in the way of my precious writing and it wasn't essential, I would say no.

I still do, by the way. I don't do breakfasts and you will rarely see me out and about lunching – both cut badly into the day. I avoid any non-essential functions that impede on my writing hours, or indeed my precious family time. I don't believe I am missing anything. Nowadays, if I want to meet someone I will make an appointment from 2 p.m. onwards when the creative part of my writing day is usually done. I'll discuss this in depth in the coming chapters.

So! When I was gearing up to submit my first manu-script fifteen years ago the publishing industry looked a whole lot different from how it does today. Publishers were a mysterious breed who lived high on mountains among the clouds: in fact they were so mythical that a new writer rarely met one and almost never spoke to one.

I certainly didn't know what one looked like. I thought they wore flowing scarves and gargled with gin and gravel. Neverthless my goal was to publish my first book with one of the major publishing houses – the 'big five' as they are sometimes called. I had to climb the mountain but how would I know which door to bang on to find the right publisher?

Simple! In 1999 I looked to my bookcase, pulled out books by my three massively favoured writers in the fantasy genre – the very genre I was attempting to enter – and noticed that each spine held the same imprint. In my mind I settled for nothing less than the publisher that appeared to be the chosen stable for that gang of writers, Robin Hobb, George RR Martin, Guy Gavriel Kay. They were with HarperCollins. That's where I needed to be. The thought of being published alongside these three luminaries of the genre in 1999 felt so exciting it inspired and fuelled me. (It didn't occur to me that HarperCollins wouldn't want to read my story.)

But there were gatekeepers, weren't there? Huge, club-wielding trolls who would never let me get through to the person who was responsible for these writers, the person who I wanted to edit my book. So I rang HarperCollins, pretended to be a journalist writing a story about publishing and simply asked the receptionist who was in charge of those particular writers. She kindly gave me the name of the editor.

I know, I know, but it was harder then! You lot have it

easy now. Publishing houses have flung open their doors to you. Back then it was a closed shop and editors were ghosts who moved in their own slipstream, so a little fib was required to get me the right name.

Anyway, now I not only knew the publishing house, I knew the individual editor who I wanted to be responsible for my story.

As you can likely already tell I envisaged that my manuscript would be accepted. I think that this is something I do in life as naturally as I breathe: I picture what I want and then I go after it. I imagine myself achieving what I'm setting out to do and suddenly the journey seems logical and not nearly so daunting. Now, I'll readily admit that life doesn't always track according to plan but having a plan is a positive approach to so many of life's challenges. The act of picturing my goal seems to map out the route to success for me. It's no different for writing novels. No one else can organise your mindset, so get it sorted from the moment you make the decision that you want to write novels. Visualise yourself finishing the book, submitting it, seeing your book published. Be an optimist!

It may not go according to the daydream – but who's to say it won't? A strong and positive mindset is the foundation for setting out on this journey. There are going to be obstacles that come along but if you remain confident and trust your instincts, then you won't fall by the wayside or have any excuse to give up.

No one can give you this positive frame of mind – it's

up to you. How you achieve it is going to differ for each of you. I did not join a writers' group or have lots of readers – personally I find it distracting and I don't need others chattering over my story and giving me lots of advice.

Let me qualify, however, that being in the company of other writers never fails to nourish me. If you can belong to a group of like-minded people, pursuing a similar dream, then I would encourage you to spend time in their midst now and then. They will recharge your optimism and buoy you if you are hitting a flat spot. I know from my commercial fiction masterclass that I host twice a year that the cohorts who remain close become a magnificent support group and cheer squad for each other. They celebrate rather than denigrate each others' successes. This sort of oxygen around your dream cannot be underestimated. However, the masterclassers are people who come together, bond fast, and desperately want to see goals being kicked from within the group. Just beware of other writing groups where members are overly competitive and nitpicking, where work tends to be torn apart and fragile confidences can be damaged as a result. If you ever find yourself attached to a know-all gang like that, leave it and run away as fast as you can.

Where was I? Ah, that's right, I knew the publishing house and the editor who I was hunting. May I remind you that this was pre-email and pre-website days? I barely knew the prerequisites of the publisher – I didn't even know that sending the first three consecutive chapters of my manuscript was desirable.

Poor Stephanie Smith – she received chapters four, seven and seventeen! What an amateur. I think I even sent a block of chocolate with my submission – not a bribe, just me being considerate because I figured everyone should have chocolate when they sit down to read a story. I think I even tied the whole thing up in a big ribbon so it looked nice. Oh dear. I was so naïve.

I can still remember the day I sent away *Betrayal*, my first manuscript. I stood in the post office for a long time wondering if I was prepared to show my work to a stranger. I found the courage to hand it over the counter but even as I did so, I recall hesitating as the man at the post office pulled it towards him with my arms still attached to the box. He laughed at me.

'What's in here, then? Gold?'

'I hope so,' was all I could mutter before we both stared at it for a horribly tense ten seconds. And then I finally let go and allowed my little bird to fly from the nest.

Here's what I learned from that time: good storytelling rarely goes unnoticed.

I did a lot of things incorrectly: my writing was far from sparkling, I didn't do enough research and I didn't look into agency representation. Fifteen years ago, if I'd not been quite so creative in how I submitted, *Betrayal* would have hit the slush pile with hundreds of other manuscripts and then be expected to shoulder its way through all the gatekeepers. From what I've gathered it did get straight to

Stephanie's desk on arrival – cheeky me – and she rightly presumed the manuscript had passed through the traditional process, which back in those days went a bit like this . . . The slush pile consisted of dozens of manuscripts that arrived each week. Each would have to patiently wait its turn to be read by one of the minions who had the power to cast it aside and stamp it for rejection. Sometimes this decision could be made in an instant – in other words in a single glance at a load of spelling errors or a too ordinary beginning, it was placed without further consideration into the pile to receive a standard rejection letter. Ploughing through the towers of submissions – remember it was all paper then – by a few assistants could take weeks. And that's why rejections often took six months or more to be returned to the hopeful creator. Stephanie assumed that someone in the reading crew had enjoyed my rollicking fantasy, despite all and any obvious flaws, had given it a big tick and passed it up the chain. In a normal situation, after being read by one of the assistants, it would have then moved to the next level of reader, who might also have seen something glinting in its depths and she might then have passed it up the line until it found its way onto the right editor's desk. Me and my little fib got the whole package unopened onto the desk of the editor I was after without any gates needing to open. Stephanie admitted to me years later that she hadn't meant to read it at the moment she did but the opening paragraphs of chapter four caught her interest as she was tidying her desk. Suddenly she was turning pages, then getting up and closing the door to her office and asking the receptionist to hold calls. She was impressed enough, despite such odd chapters, to request the whole manuscript. Despite all of its amateurishness, she believed in the work and she believed, especially, that she had a new talent on her hands, one who could spin an adventuresome, exciting tale with characters to invest in. She took it to acquisitions – without me knowing – and within a month of sending off my submission I was being offered a three-book deal.

I know I cried. If I'm truthful I never doubted myself but even so, and in spite of the fib, it was a fairytale start to a new career.

I've told you all this, not to teach you that lying gets you somewhere – although let me say that confidence is a serious boon if you possess it – no, dear reader, I share this only to lift your spirits. If your storytelling is sound and you're cluey enough to be writing what the wider audience is hungry for, be assured that an editor has every reason to look hard at you. Natural-born storytellers can always acquire the writing skills; I have been nurtured by caring editorial teams who understood that, because I was doing my apprenticeship so publicly, I needed some years and books under my belt to strengthen my writing skills.

Nevertheless – and this is the very soul of being a storyteller – the inherent skill for any new writer of popular fiction is being able to weave an emotional tale that makes addictive reading because of characters the reader can care about. I do believe storytelling is a gift, and that's something new writers may have to wrestle with. It does come easier for a few – they have the flair for it as others may have that special something that allows them to run fast, draw beautifully, capture the photo that others never saw, hear the music in their heart or the poetry that skips through their mind.

It's a whole lot easier now, of course, for new writers. Publishers are easy to meet and get to know, and are openly on the hunt for emerging talent. And writers can self-publish with relative ease these days. Vanity publishing, as it was known when I was setting out, usually occurred because a writer simply couldn't get a contract with a traditional publisher. It may have been that the writer's subject matter was a family memoir and targeted at such a small audience that it didn't warrant a big print run or offer general interest to the wider reading audience. Now there is no stigma attached to self-publishing and many writers following this path are enjoying success. It used to be expensive and while a writer would have to financially invest in themselves to go down this path, it's never been easier or cheaper to get one's own book out there.

Plus, the ebook revolution has come along in my lifetime as a writer. Who'd have thought? Even as I write this I must admit that my ebook audience is substantial. Sales are always marching higher as more readers like to take their books travelling with them on e-readers. Some read an ebook for convenience, others for eco reasons, still others because they aren't sentimental about paper books, they don't have space to store them, or because they have arthritis and holding a book upright is painful.

Many people are going to buy a digital version of this book on writing and have no reason to have a physical copy of it around.

But remember, if you love the smell of a new book and you love the tactile experience of holding a book – of turning its page or getting it signed by the author – then you must keep buying printed books as much as you do ebooks. It would be a sad day if we all looked up to find that there were no more bookstores and that the printed book had gone the way of music CDs.

That said, I'm watching several of my masterclassers win themselves wonderful opportunities with big publishers, and these big publishers are taking them into ebook format first. In today's publishing climate, it's a savvy way to get your work in front of an audience, build a profile, assemble a fan base and then, when the time is right, that same publisher can discuss taking the e-novelist into print. If you are offered this option, give it serious consideration. Don't be so narrow-minded that only traditional print will give you the publishing 'rush' you need or the stamp of approval you crave. And certainly don't listen to the internet trolls out there who claim that ebooks don't count; I curl my lip whenever I read such rubbish. Clearly they are not earning a living as novelists!

We truly have lived through a revolution in publishing.

The route to getting your name in print and the options on how you can be published are wide and varied. If you are being read by a paying audience and gathering fans along the way, then you can feel enormously chuffed.

There is no rulebook. Although it's true that adversity is a great source of inspiration for writers, you don't have to bleed for your writing. There is no formal requirement to struggle to be published, nor is it an important qualification – a badge of honour, so to speak – to have two dozen rejected manuscripts gathering dust somewhere. I refuse to feel guilty for my fairytale introduction into traditional publishing but at the same time I want to reassure emerging writers that if I can . . . then so can you!

But you do have to be prepared to work hard. You will have to develop a tough hide and a philosophical attitude, because rejection is more common than acceptance. It will be especially helpful if you come to your writing with solid business acumen and if you don't have it, then start developing your business skills. While you're at it, think about your self-promotional skills too. On top of that you do have to cultivate immense patience.

Let me assure you that Patience is not my middle name, it's not even something that shows up in my DNA. I am, in fact, a walking advertisement for impatience and all of its unpleasantness. Yet I have learned that writing is a slow-burn sort of business, and that it takes time to get established as an author. Even if you, like me, can sell your first attempt at a manuscript, it's still going to take years to start earning enough from your books to survive on and a few more beyond that to feel sufficiently secure to let go of all other income – unless it's one of those wretched 'overnight successes' that sells $50 billion's worth of copies.

So, the understanding that you're going to be happy but poor for a while should be factored into the equation of your dream, your new life, your family's best interests.

I am living testimony – and there are many like me – that you can not only earn from writing, you can earn a decent living from it, particularly if you're smart, disciplined and passionate about it. And it helps to be writing popular fiction too, so well done you on choosing to write a popular novel. Literary writers may win the tower of awards and critical acclaim yet few can sell the tower of books that some of the world's commercial fiction writers do. There's room enough for all of us. For a number of reasons I don't read a lot of literary fiction. When I do, and I choose it carefully, I love it. I hope literary writers are not dismissive of us commercial writers either, especially as I firmly believe that it's the popular fiction selling in the tens and sometimes the hundreds of thousands that permits publishers to take a risk on the beautiful prose and exquisitely crafted work of the literary authors and sell a few thousand – or a few hundred – of their works.

A lot of what I'm going to share with you is common sense. Still, sometimes it's helpful to be reminded, isn't it? I am going to work hard to keep my advice simple to follow, full of energy and down to earth . . . just like my stories.

How To Write Your Blockbuster aims to be an entirely practical guide, one that will get you started writing your popular fiction novel and setting yourself up for success.

It is all about commercial goals rather than purely personal or emotional ones. If you write just because you love it, then wonderful: keep writing, but you don't need this book. However, if you want to write to earn a crust and aren't sure how or where to begin, or you need something or someone to give you a push, then somewhere between these pages perhaps you'll find some thoughts, ideas and inspiration to get you started.

Please keep in mind that this is one person's perspective. There are no hard and fast rules to writing and I am no oracle. I've been writing popular genre fiction for fifteen years now, currently working on my thirtieth novel and I earn a comfortable living from it, so perhaps what I've learned will help you. Other writers will have different experiences and more pearls of wisdom.

This is what I have for you . . .

1.

DON'T DABBLE!

I constantly meet people who say they would love to write a book, or they intend to write a book some day, or they know someone who is thinking about writing a book or indeed that they are in the midst of writing their long-planned novel.

I admire everyone who wants to write a book. Sadly I know the majority of aspiring novelists will just talk about it. And yes, some of them will make a start and keep tinkering, often for years. Regardless, the key difference between these people and all of us who have been published is that at some point the writers in my camp stopped talking about it, stopped dreaming about it and got on with writing. We finished a manuscript with all of its trial and pain. And, even more impressively, we found the courage to send it off to a publisher or show it to an agent.

I regularly ask aspiring novelists, 'What's the worst thing that could happen if you get to this point?' Everyone replies, 'My manuscript gets rejected.' They're right. That's the most bleak it gets. But then start thinking about what the best possible outcome could be and of course it's so shiny and sparkly and exciting that it's worth all the hard work. Simply by overcoming the fear of rejection you can give your manuscript a go at the big time.

So, as an aspiring writer, you owe it to yourself to finish a manuscript and at the very least see where you can take it and what it can achieve. It may well be rejected by a publisher. Rejections aren't always due to the quality of the work; more often than you can imagine, rejections occur simply because the manuscript doesn't suit the acquisitions team *at that time*, or the publisher or agent isn't looking for that sort of story *just then*. But the needs of publishing houses, the tastes of editors and agents, even the demands of the market are fluid. The pathway to publication can change direction in a heartbeat and it does.

These shifts are affected by everything from the state of the economy to far less tangible reasons such as a theme that catches fire. One year vampires will be all the rage, the next year hot sex novels and after that it'll be anything about France. Then it's kickarse women who don't fit the mould, such as Lisbeth Salinger, the phenomenal success of *Gone Girl* – think of all the imitation book titles and covers that followed – or a trainee magician with round glasses and a scar on his forehead.

And yes, I'll grant you, most times that a rejection occurs it's because the manuscript isn't quite right yet. The writing may need finessing, the plot may still be a bit clunky or there may be characters that aren't fully developed. If that's the case then hopefully the acquisitions team has done you a favour and drawn your attention to what needs improving and you can learn from that submission.

If you find yourself with a generic rejection letter and no constructive feedback, then it's on to another publisher or agent. If you have too many blanket rejections and no feedback from publishers or agents, then you have to turn your sights back to the manuscript and understand that something isn't right about it. It could just be the genre – I know a very capable writer who was recently rejected because the publishers couldn't quite marry up the genres she was combining. When that happens, it's harder for them to see their way forward to making it a winner within the wider audience. They liked the story and liked the writing, but it was neither one thing nor the other. It must have been frustrating for her but at least she had that information to work with. Without the feedback she would have had to rely on her own instincts and her network of readers to clue her in as to what wasn't working about the manuscript.

Whatever the reason for rejection, you've achieved the amazing milestone of finishing a manuscript and going through the process of submitting it for consideration. It's hard, damn hard to send it out into the world! It's scary and it's fraught – you're exposing yourself and your writing and you may feel insecure about that. But it must be done if you're going to hit the big stage. All of us who are partnered up with a publishing house have fought this battle and at some point emerged victorious – but *only* because we finished what we began.

So your primary goal when you set out is to finish the manuscript. You may well lose puff halfway through, or become disillusioned or uncertain. It doesn't matter! At this stage no one has seen it but you. Finish it! And even if you don't show it to another soul, get yourself into the habit of finishing each project you begin. This professional approach is going to be one of the cornerstones you lay for your future as a writer. I have a close friend who is a beautiful writer. He has no ambition to have a novel published. He doesn't need any acclaim for his work other than the smiles and round of applause he receives at his local writing group in a very small town. He writes hordes of short stories, gets the most enormous kick out of producing them, loves his friends sharing them and especially enjoys performing them. But ask him about getting them published or writing a novel and he squirms. That's not his bag. But Tony finishes his stories: that's what is admirable. If he ever changes his mind and decides to submit his work, he'll be ready to go. And if a publisher says, 'Yes please,' he'll be a reliable novelist.

School yourself to finish what you begin or you will remain one of those people I mentioned at the beginning:

one who talks a great deal about writing and dabbles a lot in writing but doesn't actually push a project along to completion.

WHY DO SO MANY DABBLERS EXIST?

Dabblers are invariably earnest writers who work hard at their craft and, even if they have no great ambition to be novelists on the world stage, they write, write, write. They write for so many different reasons. They might be natural-born storytellers or have a story idea that has great potential as a piece of fiction. Then there are all those people who want to delve into their family history and write a memoir. Many write about their negative childhood experiences or failed relationships because it's cathartic to let it out onto the page. Some people are experts in their field and feel moved to write about the wisdom they've acquired, whether it's in the field of cookery, gardening, knitting – a host of hobbies and professions, in fact.

At the root of all this is a desire to share. Most often we not only hear a story in our minds, we can see it unfurling, almost like we are watching it in motion. It's natural to want other people to see that story too. Sometimes it's hard to know where to begin if you're tackling your first manuscript and for others it's just hard to know where the story itself best begins.

Frequently people try to bring their story to life on the page but allow life to get in the way: they lose track of their tale, run out of steam and give up. And some dabblers become lost in the process wrestling the story they have in their mind into an entertaining piece of written material. Daunted, they stop writing for a while or shift to another story they've been dabbling with.

Time and again I have writers turning up at my workshops feeling frustrated and looking for inspiration or some sort of catalyst to kickstart them on a beautiful story-writing pathway. They want to craft their novel in the time frame that I do and have all the architecture of their story coming together with less angst, more fluidity. Mostly they're wondering if there's some magic ingredient they're lacking that I can give them.

The only ingredient I possess is discipline – the commitment to finish the project.

There are dabblers who arrive at the masterclass who are feeling disillusioned. They want to write, they have stories knocking around in their minds. When I ask them directly why they feel they aren't getting anywhere, I am hit with an array of excuses, all of them valid enough. They can range from 'I've got a lot of work on at the moment' to 'Well, I've got children' to everything in between.

Now those reasons are perfectly sound – if you're a dabbler.

However, if you're committed to a writing career, then these reasons are nothing more than lame excuses. The majority of successful novelists I know – and by successful I'm applying earning power as the criteria – are parents, are husbands and wives, are perhaps holding down another full-time job and are certainly running their own business as full-time writers. They're at writing workshops and hosting seminars. They're visiting schools and libraries. They're on tour, getting to festivals, giving keynote speeches at literary luncheons or sitting on panels at various events. They're meeting booksellers and dropping in on book groups. They're driving dozens of kilometres just to do a small signing in a shopping centre because the local bookshop there has been so supportive. They're doing dozens of tasks – just like you – to keep their household ticking along and their families contented, and all the while they're juggling many other jobs associated with the business of writing without actually adding a single word to their manuscript. And then, on top of all of this, they're writing and producing finished drafts to go off to their editors.

Novelists who earn a good living from their books do not give themselves excuses. I wrote my first manuscript as a married mum with twin sons at junior primary while running a business with my husband; I did all my writing late at night while the house slept. The only person who missed out on anything in our household was me – I missed out on sleep and social events. But I did so because once I'd decided I was going to write my first novel, I became entirely committed to finishing the first draft.

So when the excuses are being rolled out, I mentally roll my eyes. The only justifications I can accept are serious interruptions to one's daily life such as illness – and that doesn't mean colds and coughs. Please, harden up! A new baby, moving house, emergencies . . . that's the sort of major event I'm referring to. Everything else is simply daily life and you have to work it out, cope with it, make time for your writing and stop giving yourself permission not to finish what you've begun.

HOW TO STOP BEING A DABBLER
OR A BABBLER

The first box you need to tick is to stop talking about your writing and get on with it. Set yourself up to succeed by achieving the following.

Get your family on side

Inform them of your plan to write a novel. You want them to take your work seriously enough that they won't derail your efforts. Most importantly, they need to understand what you need from them.

Writers need quiet. Writers need a quiet space. Writers need a quiet space and time. Writers need a quiet space and time – alone. *Alone!*

So work out a routine that fits your family. No two routines are alike because each of us is an individual and our families are unique. However, if you work normal business hours, then the chances are that your writing is going to be done either early morning or in the evening. Add children to the mix and it's likely that you'll be writing much later in the evening as I did. Some of you may be in the position where you don't have to work or raise children – you have even less sympathy from me in terms of your available time. Don't waste that quiet time in the house.

For those who have an infant or two, take your chances when they sleep or if you need to rest then, make sure you write when they finally go down for the night. I know single parents will find the workload tough. It is tough! No one said this is going to be easy. But no complaints please as no one's forcing you to take up writing.

If you are a single parent with a new baby in the house, it's probably wise to put your writing plans on hold until you have established regular sleep patterns. Otherwise, you are going to be a wreck. Baby comes first and so does the health and wellbeing of any other members of your family. The writing will wait, the baby's next feed won't. Use the time to dream, to plan, to think about characters or storylines – and to read! Your baby will be six months old, eating solids and sleeping through the night before you can blink.

Don't steal time from your family. They need you – and you need them. They are your cheer squad, and from them you'll draw your smiles and inspiration when the going gets tough, as it will. Lavish your family with the love and attention it needs to thrive. Steal time only from yourself.

Give up television and the internet

You will never get a manuscript written if you zone out habitually to banal viewing. No harm in tuning in to your favourite programs. If you watch quality drama it will enrich your storytelling. I have my favourite programs but I turn them on just as the theme music begins and switch them off as soon as the program ends. Don't watch programs either side of your favourites and don't ever turn that TV on unless there's something specific that you really want to watch.

Now, worse than television is social media. Facebook, Twitter and Instagram are dominating a huge chunk of many people's lives. I like Facebook and I have no problem with social media – especially because of the way in which it connects everyone. And I have made use of social media for everything from marketing my books to mobilising thousands of people to help me with a particular cause, so I am not criticising it. I am, however, daunted by its potential to work against you.

As a writer, social media is your competitor in two ways.

It's a time vampire. Really, how many thoughts for the day does one need to have? How many photos of other people's children or grandchildren do you need to like? How often do you really need to be scrolling through your home page? How about limiting yourself to a certain number of visits per day? What about twice? Three at the most. No need to have it constantly open and distracting you with trivial stuff and there is so much trivia – some people surely sit behind their computers all day with an eye on Facebook and feel obliged to share their every thought or feeling. Don't be sucked in – read what's fun, relevant to you, enriching to you. Most of it is flotsam and jetsam you can do without when you are writing your novel. Tweet strategically but don't linger or get lost in a mire of information.

I know how much time Facebook and Twitter – the social media I use regularly – drag from my day, so I am strict about how often I visit the sites. If I wasn't strict I could easily get sucked into a spiral of information that doesn't add anything relevant to my life or educate me. So I'm strategic and directed: I go in and get out swiftly. I make sure I attend to my page, to all enquiries and comments, and then I'm gone. This discipline ensures my writing time isn't thieved by Facebook or Twitter.

The second way that social media competes with you as a writer is because the novel you're so keen to sell and have published will have to jostle for attention against the juggernaut of social media. It's arresting to discover how many people spend hours on social media when they could be reading a great book – *your* book.

Make sacrifices in your social life

Explain to your friends what you're doing.

At first they probably won't take you entirely seriously. That's okay; at the moment it can't be viewed as anything other than a hobby because unless you have a contract, it remains a dream. That said, do show the people around you that you're determined to follow that dream. Don't blame them for not placing the same importance on the writing of your novel as you do. The best suggestion I have here is to demonstrate writing's importance to you by being busy with it – they'll get the message soon enough. And until that message gets through remain cheerful and gentle when you turn down invitations. In this way you are showing your commitment to your hobby. Family and friends will become accustomed to the fact that you are not available for every get together. More importantly, perhaps they'll grasp that they can't just drop around the way they used to because you are now working on your novel and unannounced visits are disruptive.

The trick, of course, is not to become precious about your novel. Once you do that you're a total drag to be around. Your novel is not important to anyone but you, so don't try to make it anything but that. Let it sit in your heart, dominate your thoughts if it must and even rampage through your dreams but avoid bleating that no one is taking it seriously and avoid desperately trying to make everyone care about it as much as you do. They don't! Committing to your novel is your task, not theirs. It's also your choice, so don't make it anyone else's burden.

Be honest about when you're working on your novel
Set up some boundaries that everyone can become accustomed to. If you're someone who works from home,

then your friends and family may already be trained not to come calling. However, if you're perhaps taking a few months off to write, using precious holiday weeks, taking a sabbatical or even retiring from work, then your circle of friends needs to understand that you're still working when you're sitting at your home desk and tapping away at the keyboard. In fact you're still working when you sit back and stare into space for a minute or two.

I had a hard time convincing some people that I was working when I stopped going into an office in the city and began to work on novels at home. I was earning my living from writing – our family was depending on me to make this new career work – but there were people who thought it was okay to just drop around. 'Shall we have a cuppa? I won't stay long' was a regular catchcry. Arghhh! Be firm, the answer is no.

Respect your own working hours

This brings me to home offices. Anyone who has one – and runs a business from it – will know how many interruptions occur that can derail you from your course. This is especially tricky for writers, who have to build a bubble around themselves in order to construct the worlds for their readers to enter: whether it's Paris, the outback or another world entirely. If you have the luxury of being able to designate a room as your home office from which you can write, then consider it purely a place of work. And while you're in it make sure you *do* work; don't leap up to put on a wash, clear out a messy cupboard or weed the garden beds. Don't duck out to the supermarket or the bank. It's easy to do because you're at home, just as it's easy to stop for a break if a friend drops around. But these interruptions – if you permit them – destroy your mindset. They will chip away at your allocated writing hours and suddenly it will be time to pick up the children or start the dinner and you'll beat yourself up because a working day has slipped by. I'm all about taking down time, let me add. It's extremely healthy to spend time away from the keyboard and screen. The back of the brain takes care of business while you're cooking, cleaning, exercising, running errands and all those other chores that you have to do to keep your life and your family ticking along. But if you commit to a writing session don't let anything interrupt the time you've made for it.

While it's okay at the beginning for everyone else to think of your writing as a hobby, you must think of yourself as a writer. It's important to embrace the notion and approach it professionally because until you do, everyone around you will struggle to. I'm not suggesting you scream it from the rooftops but find the courage to make sacrifices, establish a routine and respect your working hours. This is a major step forward.

2.

BEFORE YOU BEGIN

WRITE WHAT YOU KNOW AND WHAT YOU LOVE TO READ

Other writers will tell you to write what you know. This has dual meaning. First and foremost what they're saying is to write what you understand. Everyone's experience of the world is wildly different – from our background, family and culture, to the jobs we've done, the children we've raised and the people we've known. Some people are farmers, some are brain surgeons and others drive taxis. There are a host of careers that expose individuals to different experiences and life events. Obviously someone who has grown up in rural Australia is going to write from the heart a lot easier about life on an Australian farm than someone who grew up in London's East End.

I'm exaggerating to make my point. But perhaps I can

make it clearer by offering a real example. Around 2006 I was writing adult fantasy fiction and forging a career in the fantasy genre. A writer friend, successful in the same genre, admitted to envying me my childhood in Britain. He grasped that I just seemed to get the whole ancient history thing and that for me writing about medieval times with castles and baileys, kings and queens, pomp and pageantry was second nature. It came to me easily. It was in my soul almost. Meanwhile he inherently understood the harsh sun on dry earth, the brightest blue skies, vast desolate spaces and crashing surf on golden beaches, ancient wilderness, virgin land, tropical rainforest to rivers with prehistoric predators in their depths. Until he mentioned this, I'd never fully understood the notion that I was writing what I knew and therefore writing what came naturally to me.

And now that I look back over my novels, I see that all of them are written with that Eurocentric skew, one that references, time and again, my upbringing in Britain. Childhood is a time of vivid memories and I see now that that is evident in my writing. I am writing what I know.

The 'write what you know' advice can be applied in another way: write what you love to read. If you love to read crime, for example, then you'll know what crime readers are looking for when they buy a novel – the tropes and conventions, the structure of the tale, the sorts of characters and plot lines that make the best crime reading. And that, of course, follows through into each genre. Readers of fantasy, readers of romance, readers of thrillers or chick lit or sci-fi – they all have specific expectations that you must fulfil in order to please, to keep your audience coming back for more.

If you don't understand what each genre's audience likes, then you're at a disadvantage. And if you are not a crime reader and you're about to tackle a crime manuscript, then I'd suggest you start devouring some of the best quality and bestselling practitioners of the genre as soon as possible.

There's no reason why a fantasy reader can't write a thumping romance – no reason at all. But respect your audience. Make sure that you know what they want from you. This is commercial fiction, remember – it must sell! The audience demands and gets what it wants from publishers.

Continuing with a crime thriller as our example, note that the reader is not looking for an angsty book about lost love. Crime readers are discerning and they're loyal once they find an author they enjoy. Work out what sort of crime you're going to write. Is it a whodunnit or a police procedural? Is it gritty urban crime or a cosy crime? Is it hardboiled, a spy mystery or noir? Perhaps it's a legal drama or, my favourite, a psychological thriller.

Every genre has subgenres. Romance subgenres range from historical to paranormal; fantasy embraces a seemingly endless array from the epic quest to steampunk.

Know as much as you can about the genre you want to write in. This will ensure that you're clued in to the trends and commercial possibilities of the genre and you'll have a sense of what the acquisitions editor or agent will be looking for.

There are fads in fiction – Stieg Larsson and J K Rowling taught us that.

Mainstream fiction appeals to the widest possible audience – that's men, women and youngsters who can crossover and enjoy an adult read.

Fashions come and go. If the genre you're writing into is already a fad then you may be too late to ride that wave of success. Take a look at what you like to read, investigate who is writing in that genre and, finally research what sort of market there is for the writers of that style of story.

It's wise to analyse what is out there and what is selling and why.

It certainly pays to know what people are gobbling up if you want to take a highly commercial approach to your writing. But, for argument's sake, even if fantasy is hot, hot, hot and showing no sign of cooling, please don't write it for the sake of cashing in. If you don't read it, don't go there. And as crazy as it sounds, even if fantasy is one of the more popular genres to read in any given year, it doesn't necessarily mean that publishers are going to be acquiring it. My reading of the industry is that publishers in this area have been looking to the hugely popular and well-established writers of fantasy and have not been highly active in acquiring new talent in the genre. So, there's another reason to analyse the market. Know what are people reading and learn what publishers are acquiring.

If you don't read it, you don't know how to write it – not yet.

So, first piece of homework. Read the most popular writers in the genre – they didn't achieve that sales record or that level of popularity by writing ordinary stuff. They sell in the hundreds of thousands because people around the world love their work. Give your audience your full respect by reading their favourite works. Analyse them, work out how the writers structure their tales, learn about pacing and dialogue, plots and popular themes. We'll discuss the technical points later but the order of business is for you to know your genre inside and out. You may take five years to finish your first manuscript, so there's no point in trying to ride a fad if that wave has already passed through by the time you're ready.

Understand the settings that work best for your chosen genre. If it's commercial romance you want to write, then know which environments are being enjoyed by readers and project forward. Is it historical or contemporary? Is it rural or urban? Is it real or fantastical? It's especially important to keep in mind the time frame in which your book might hit the publisher's acquisitions meeting.

When I was ready to show an editor my first manuscript I knew HarperCollins was on the hunt for new writers of the epic fantasy, high fantasy and heroic fantasy sub-genres. At the time, the publisher was actively looking for homegrown writers who could leap aboard the fantasy juggernaut that was promising to gain momentum locally.

Throughout the early 1990s I'd been gobbling up the works of George R R Martin, Robin Hobb, Guy Gavriel Kay and Tad Williams – not to mention the dozen other top writers of the time – and they were all North American or British. Publishers were beginning to acquire these authors while booksellers were beginning to stock them and I could see the genre exploding. I loved reading fantasy and it seemed natural that when I attempted to write a novel it would be an epic fantasy series. But you see, I'd done my homework. I produced a manuscript that suited precisely that category, doing my utmost to hit the right notes, the notes that were quickening that genre's pulse in the ANZ market. And when you love reading fantasy, for instance, writing a pulse-pounding epic fantasy feels right rather than being a struggle. Why? Because you are writing what you love to read.

I gave myself the very best chance of being picked up by the then Australian leader of fantasy fiction publishing. My editor was my champion and she was determined to win approval in the boardroom for this manuscript. The story's premise, its arc, its characters and the writing had already ticked the right boxes. By the time I got to this stage, dear writer, it really was all down to luck and timing. There was a budget available, the right editor available, right publishing date free, right 'publishing mindset' in place within the company, plus we had booksellers keen for fantasy and a reading audience hungry for the genre. Luck and fate conspired to bring all this together so once my novel *Betrayal* had the backing of Australia's most senior, talented and respected editor in fantasy fiction, it was only a matter of those gathered at the meeting to simply nod their heads and say, 'Go to offer'.

In today's fast-moving world, manuscripts are rarely submitted in the mail as printed parcels of promise, as mine was in the year 2000. Within a decade I was whizzing my 140 000-word manuscripts down a cable via an invisible, magical network of beeps and whirrs that miraculously took it from my screen to my publisher's screen in a few heartbeats. Gosh, the internet was exciting back then! Today authors tend to email cover letters together with a synopsis and sample chapters or completed manuscript. But how you come to find that elusive person to send it to can depend on the whim of the heavens.

Editors come via stories in myriad ways – at festivals, through agents, at bookish events and via other authors' recommendations. Now many local publishers have flung open their doors to the public and are inviting new writers to pitch their unsolicited manuscripts. Submission information is readily available on their websites, making it easier for the first-time writer to sharpen their application.

Editors also hear about great new talent through literary agents, through writing competitions and indeed from their overseas offices.

It goes without saying that publishers want to maintain strong relationships with their successful authors so that they can go back to the well and discuss the other projects they have on the boil.

There is no proven way to attract the attention of an editor but you can certainly do lots of homework to ensure that you target the right person at the publishing house that will best suit your manuscript. If you don't do the research, you're bonkers – there is so much information available online. Find out who publishes what and why. If your work can sit strongly alongside my stories, for instance, then you should be actively hunting down who my editor is and the publishing company that she works for. You would then be checking that publisher's website for submission guidelines and whether it offers any pitching opportunities for new writers without agents.

So, in summary:
- Know your genre and understand where your story sits in the market. Read widely in your genre: whether it's fantasy, sci-fi, romance, historical, crime, thriller. Remember, every genre has conventions that its readers enjoy – they're the reasons they choose to read it.
- Learn who reads that sort of genre. Is it women? A cross-section of male and female? Is it middle-aged people? The more you learn about your market the better you will be able to target your story. And the more you know about your readership, the better the world that you create will be.
- Read as much as you can in the genre you want to

write in so you can approach your own manuscript and its submission in the most professional manner. The best way to learn is to read the top writers in the genre you love and, particularly, the subgenre you are leaning towards. Quality bookshops have assistants who read extensively and know the genres and their tropes. Ask them for advice on the top six writers you should be reading.

- If you know which genre you're going to write in because you read it with joy yourself, then half the battle is won. Now you just have to write a fantastic story, just for you – the sort of tale that you are prepared to pay good money for and then invest your precious spare hours into.

FINDING THE RIGHT STORY – WHERE DOES THE IDEA COME FROM?

Okay, now you know the genre you want your story to fit into but how do you know what story to write?

Where does the inspiration for stories come from?

The question 'Where do you get your ideas from?' is the most feared item during any author's Q&A session. We know it's coming – it's always asked by someone. Some of the time it's asked to kickstart the Q&A session but mostly it's asked in earnest by an aspiring writer who wants to be shown the wellspring.

It's a perfectly logical and legitimate request but the

problem for me and for many writers I know is that there is no straightforward answer to that question. Ideas don't come from just the one place.

There's always a trigger. We may have read an article or seen a documentary. Something has caught our attention on the internet, or someone has told us an anecdote or recounted a particular experience. Sometimes the spark comes from our own lives but more often than not the seed of a story is given to us by an outside source. We water it and nourish it and look after it and that seed grows and flourishes into a full-blown tale because we've added our imagination and our life experiences to it. It may even be a series of ideas blending and working together. Essentially, stories for novels are drawn from everyday life.

That's not helping you, is it? Much too vague, right? Sigh. I know. I warned you, we don't really know.

EXERCISE

If you're frowning or lost for an idea, try this exercise, designed to open your mind to ideas.

1. Get out a piece of blank paper. In the middle of the page write down a negative emotion. Write the first emotion that comes to mind. Perhaps it's connected with the anxiety of not knowing where to find the right idea for your story.

2. Draw a circle around that word. I'm going to choose the word 'fear' as an example but I expect you'll have other words that bubble up.

3. Now draw a line radiating out of the central circle and at the end of the line write the first word you think of that's associated with your chosen emotion. For me, the word that comes to mind after fear is 'huntsman'.

4. Keep drawing lines from the central word and, without forcing it, write down every word or phrase that you associate with your negative emotion. Fear may spawn not only huntsman spiders but loneliness, death, lost children, heights, flying, bombs, bills, injury, disease, and so on and so forth. It doesn't matter if it's random. For instance, the word bomb could lead you to think of Europe, a lone woman traveller, why is she there, what's she doing to be caught up in a bombing and the inevitable, 'What happened next?'

   Hopefully you will end up with a page that looks like the spokes of a bicycle wheel, with dozens of words and phrases emanating from the original negative emotion.

   The exercise is quite enlightening up to this point alone as it tends to drive away inhibitions and loosens up your creative juices to think randomly, broadly, imaginatively.

5. Now choose a single word or phrase from the collection on your bicycle spokes that speaks to you strongly. I'm going to choose 'loneliness' for the sake of this exercise. Place a

second piece of paper in front of you and write at the top in large letters your chosen word or phrase. Now answer the following questions:

- Who is experiencing the problem associated with the word at the top of the page?
- Why are they experiencing it?
- When are they experiencing it?
- Where are they experiencing it?
- What is causing it? What can they do about it? What might come next?

6. Suddenly – once you've answered the who, the why, the when, the where and the what – you'll have the seed of a story idea. It doesn't have to be *the* burning white-hot idea that is going to form the basis of your first bestseller but at least it's proved to you that stories can come from the simplest of triggers – as simple as a word on a page.

7. You can take the negative emotion exercise further still by asking yourself the 'what if' question. Apply it as follows:

- What if a *lonely* woman decides to take off on a whirlwind holiday to Europe to find friendship among the romantic landscape of the Italian riviera?
- What if a man involved in an accident that kills his children is driven by *loneliness* and despair to walking the streets at night and gets involved with homeless youth?
- What if a *lonely* girl goes hunting for romance in London and disappears?

To finish up on the ideas question, it's fair to add that the more books I publish, the more strategic I become about writing them and this is likely the case for most busy commercial novelists. I'm always thinking several projects ahead. It's a habit that has evolved naturally. I'm positive that it will happen for you too because, like me, you'll develop a new radar for potential stories. What I mean by that is that I am paying more attention to the world around me: to conversations, to events, to odd news items. I'm also reading books of nonfiction – a place from which a lot of the great ideas for fiction are found.

I already know the theme and rough storyline of the next three novels I will write. I know the setting and its era. I don't know much about the cast of characters or even where the story will go but I know my main character and what his or her struggles are. The rest will come. There's no need to question the universe – the universe delivers. Just focus on the story you currently have whispering in your imagination and, invariably you'll see that, as you begin to write it the next idea will wave to you from the horizon. If anything, you'll have to demonstrate discipline not to wave back until the current project is done.

In light of that suggestion, do what I do now and start paying attention to the world around you.

Fourteen or so years ago I was breezing through my days, really only taking notice of stuff that was relevant to my own life. Now I possess a radar that is always scanning for the next great idea.

I notice how birds sound and move. I see how trees actually look when they sway in the breeze rather than how I think they may appear. I spend plenty of time staring at the sky and noticing it at different times of the day, month and year. I watch how clouds move in different weather patterns. Its sounds obvious, I know, but are you doing it? Are you paying attention to the tones in people's voices or their style of walking, their various mannerisms? Do you notice how smells can trigger images?

There is the potential for a story in everything you hear about, read about and listen to.

Betrayal was my first book and its theme emerged because I was going through IVF, which was ultimately successful with a twin pregnancy. At thirteen weeks, after a traumatic Saturday in my bathroom, I was told I'd lost one of our precious children. But when they checked for a heartbeat on the remaining twin, they found two solid heartbeats. My husband and I were deliriously happy but quietly confused. The medical team came to the conclusion that I'd lost a triplet – a child that none of us had known about, one that had been near invisibly growing in my womb. At the time I was so overjoyed and grateful to the universe that the babies we knew about were safe, hearts beating strongly, that I didn't allow myself any grief.

A few years later with healthy twin sons and a new fire in my belly – this time to write a fantasy novel, I began writing about everything in threes. My books had the series title of Trinity. I was writing a trilogy. The book was about three children and there was even a trio of magical talismans. It was a shock when I realised much later that this was likely a subconscious ode to the little one who got away. I believe I channelled my grief at the loss of a child, and the loss of a sibling for our boys, into my storytelling.

My editor pointed out that I like to write about love triangles in my non-fantasy novels and that was a surprise too. The subconscious is a wonderful and puzzling spirit within – here it is, still imbuing my stories with that connection to the number three from nearly a quarter of a century ago.

The next series I wrote was called The Quickening and comprised *Myrren's Gift*, *Blood and Memory* and *Bridge of Souls*. It arrived because of a simple story about a visit to a clairvoyant that a friend shared with me in passing. To Di her story was just an anecdote to fill a long drive. To me it was gold. Her clairvoyant conveyed to her that she had apparently passed through many lives and had brought with her lots of experiences. When Di asked the seer why she wasn't aware of her past, the clairvoyant assured her that it didn't work that way, that each new life she lived was unburdened by the previous lives, other than her accumulated wisdom.

Well! My friend's chatter faded to background noise as my imagination began to run with the notion of being born again except I twisted the idea into something more sinister. The idea of reincarnation quickly transformed in my mind as stealing someone else's life. And that was like an explosion in my thoughts. How could someone steal a life? I recalled how terrified I was by *The Exorcist* in my teens and the hideously unnerving movie of the same name, the movie that I couldn't get through. I think I even burned the book because its presence in my life terrified me. Yes, a demon could steal someone's life. Poor Di was still talking and I was beginning to press harder on the accelerator as my excitement built around the seed of this new story. What if I didn't want demons but I wanted a normal, likeable person to possess another normal, likeable person? Yes! I yelled inwardly, gripping the steering wheel harder, pressing slightly more forcefully on the right pedal. What if the possessor has no idea he can do this? What if he's cursed and can't die but has to inhabit other lives against his will as he desperately searches for answers? Yes, yes, yes! I had it. The story was mine. He's a young man, in a position of power, a decent fellow with a grand future but he dies young on the order of his enemy. What his enemy doesn't know is that our hero has a terrible magic – sinister and silent, it manifests itself many years later in the most chilling of ways: to steal lives.

The Quickening is the story that took my name and books onto the global stage so I didn't mind paying that eye-wateringly large speeding fine that the policeman waiting on the side road slapped into my hand as I approached the Clare Valley.

The third series, Percheron, began with *Odalisque*, followed by *Emissary* and then *Goddess*. It arose because of a dusty old book my husband gave me about the Ottoman Empire and its amazing royal harem. 'Here, read this,' he said one day while rummaging through a pile of family books from his great-aunt's library. I ignored it for a while but to keep the peace I decided to glance through it. I can clearly remember how my breathing slowed and I began to tune out to all other sounds. I was suddenly in a new world. I was in eleventh century Constantinople in the golden age of the Ottomans when their power and riches were at their height. The book was extraordinarily detailed and based on the discoveries of a seventeenth century traveller who managed to get behind closed doors of the Topkapi Palace. I was immersed, entranced, fascinated and I read it cover to cover in one session.

'Brilliant, isn't it?' my husband remarked after I finally looked up many hours later. He was offering me a cup of tea. 'Some great stories in there.'

Great stories? It had everything I dreamed of for a fresh and unique piece of fantasy storytelling, and it had fallen into my lap. My resulting story entailed a beautiful young woman sold to the royal palace as an odalisque for a new Zar and her struggles with the Zar's ambitious and controlling mother. It was a hotbed of thrills and drama to write about, including several three-way relationships!

The next series comprising *Royal Exile*, *Tyrant's Blood* and *King's Wrath* came into being because I was visiting Wales and was inspired by the ruins of a castle in its north. Walking those walls I felt history clawing up through my feet and begging to be noticed, especially the stories of its once proud princes – sovereigns in their own right – who had ruled over Wales and irritated the English royals no end. My journey to that fortress with its many secrets, including a hidden tunnel, inspired the Valisar trilogy and the entire half-million-word series that followed. Once I had an ingress, a secret hallway, in my mind, I began to feel that it might be the haunt of a curious child, one who happens to be in the ingress when catastrophe hits and the castle is invaded. From there I spun an epic tale of treachery, revenge, love and disaster.

When I turned to writing crime, the first story came from delving back into my teenage years. In truth it was simply the time and the setting in my life that triggered the story. This happens frequently for me. I visit a place – like the fortress at Conwy or Bridestowe Lavender Farm in Tasmania – and I feel that inner radar beeping madly at me, telling me that this place will deliver me a story if I dwell on it. This was the case with *Bye Bye Baby*, my first attempt at a crime novel. It was when I was back in my birthplace England, walking through Hove Park, a park that I used to play in as a youngster – these were simpler times when teenagers used to discuss angst on the swings or the slide! – the memories of the smells and sounds, the cars on the road, the whole Brighton seafront scene came to life for me. This moment was followed by a visit to Scotland Yard, where a senior policeman gave me a brilliant guided tour, allowing me to venture behind the scenes into places where the public was rarely allowed (not even other novelists!). Those two experiences sealed the deal for me. I would write a crime novel using all this bristling memory of the sixties and this glance in to the life of contemporary Scotland Yard. The character of DCI Jack Hawksworth built himself but the story's trauma was inspired by the notion of how a cold case never stops troubling the police men and women involved in it. The plot was entirely from my imagination.

The second book in the Jack Hawksworth series is *Beautiful Death* and it arose from an article I read on the internet about pioneering medicine. You may recall the stunning news of the French woman who received a new face after her own was badly torn during a dog attack. It was the first recorded partial face transplant surgery and the news was a sensation. Around the same time, news was raging about people being either tricked into giving up their kidneys or otherwise choosing to sell them and other body parts for an inordinately high price. Harvesting human organs was big news and I learned that there was a black market for everything from kidneys to skin and bone. It was so macabre I couldn't leave it alone. Coupled with the partial face transplant breakthrough I began to think about the darker side of the medical fraternity and the corruption within. It led me down the chilling path to write *Beautiful Death*.

My historical sagas followed on from my career of fantasy writing – including six children's books – and crime novels. During my week in Hobart at the Bryce Courtenay Fiction Masterclass, I remember giving the maestro a glimpse into the story I had first hoped to write when I returned home. It was based on tales and myths within my large Anglo-Indian family that is scattered throughout the world and as child we were told these wonderful stories of life in India. My mother was one of seven, my father one of three – all of whom married and had their own families – so between all those brothers and sisters were a host of first, second and third cousins who visited. And no one realised, not even I, that growing up in our midst was a youngster who would absorb all these stories of life in India during the thirties and forties and want to explore some of them in a novel one day. Bryce listened, fascinated, and when I was done talking, he took my hand and said, 'You are not to write that story'. I looked back aghast. 'Not yet,' he explained. 'You're not ready yet. Not nearly ready to handle that novel.'

'When will I be ready?'

'You'll know,' he answered.

It was cryptic but he was right. It took me a decade and around nineteen novels before I understood not only that I was ready to tackle the family saga but that I had needed to do that public apprenticeship – that ten years of learning my craft on the job. *Fields of Gold* was worth waiting for because I was able to breathe far more life and colour, texture and sensory information into my story. I was able to evoke Cornwall of the 1920s and southern India of the

1930s within that whole Anglo-Indian culture. Of course if I wrote it now, half a dozen years down the track and another small tower of books in the vault since, I could probably write it even better.

And *Fields of Gold* opened up a doorway into a whole new world of storytelling: the mainstream women's fiction world embraced me kindly and gave me a new playground. I am humbled by its scope and that I'm only limited by my imagination.

Ideas have roared at me ever since I tasted some success with *Fields of Gold*. Imagine my delight at discovering that the Bridestowe Lavender Farm in Tasmania – so pretty, so unexpected and so deeply romantic – has its historic roots firmly in the alpine lavender fields of Provence. I had stumbled across this wonderful spot not far from Launceston, looking for somewhere to tour with my parents. Reading about the farm's history gave me that jolt of wide-eyed pleasure that usually comes with an idea for a story. The feeling soon settles in my gut and then, like a sparkling crystal, it glints and winks at me from deep within, demanding to be brought out, admired, polished and given its moment in the sunlight. The fact that the lavender mother stock of Bridestowe came from Provence was exciting but it wasn't enough; the story needed more oxygen and that was delivered with a timely visit to France and the discovery that I was arriving on the seventieth an-niversary of the liberation of Paris. I needed nothing more, the two ideas collided magnificently in my imagination.

What if – you see, that 'what if' question often arrives first in my mind – a lavender farmer in Provence, despairing of his beloved country being invaded and occupied, refuses to work for the Nazi regime and instead walks off his land and becomes a freedom fighter? He uses lavender seeds as his talisman for survival, vowing one day to plant them on a sun-scorched earth and walk the fields of his lavender in peacetime. Of course I would bring my lavender keeper from France and eventually to Australia and the wartime backdrop added so much adventure and tension to the story. It felt perfect. It was so good, in fact, and became such a big story that I had to write it over two books. *The French Promise* was the sequel.

The idea for another of my other historical sagas *Nightingale* came from within my husband's family. He told me about a young man, just twenty, who volunteered during the call to the action from England for soldiers during the First World War. Darcy joined the Light Horse, trained in Egypt, thought he'd be sent to Europe where all the action was but found his troop leaving their horses behind in Cairo and sailing to the southern tip of Turkey to a place called Gallipoli. He gave his life at Lone Pine. While I didn't want to tamper with Darcy's memory, a visit to Gallipoli confirmed I did want to write a sweeping tale of a British nurse and a South Australian Lighthorseman who meet and fall in love under extraordinary circumstances. It's an epic love story and it shows the hopelessness of war from both sides – I was determined to also share the

Turkish story of how it felt to be invaded and of the need to defend the land that one loves. This is all because of a tiny, grainy old photo that Ian had on his desk, a photo that I picked up and bothered to discover more about.

I could go but hopefully you're getting the idea that stories come from people, places, events; I've shared all of this to showcase that stories swirl around us and the key to finding your next idea for a story is just to pay attention. There are, of course, the stories that live within you. To find these you must delve into your inner self – they'll be thrilled when you discover them patiently awaiting you.

HOW MUCH DO YOU NEED TO KNOW ABOUT YOUR STORY?

Writers arrive at their manuscript wired in a host of ways.

At one end of the spectrum is the person I call 'the planner'. This is the writer who makes comprehensive notes about every aspect of his or her story – down to individual scenes and characters' backstories. The writer may not use the knowledge that one of their characters was bullied as a child, for instance, or butters their bread outwards, but the fact that they know this comforts them in their writing and helps them as they develop that particular character. These writers usually know their story's beginning, middle and end, and they're on a journey of knowledge, so to speak. By the time they actually sit down to write the tale, so much of the story has already been plotted out that they are in a position to join the dots.

These are the people who use yellow Post-it notes, whiteboards and even index cards.

The gang at the other end of this spectrum, which is where I lurk, know almost nothing about the story. I have no idea of scenes. I don't know where my story begins, let alone what happens in the middle and I definitely, absolutely never know the ending. As a result I have no genuine plan for where the story may go or how it will take shape.

I call writers with my affliction 'the freefallers'. We leap off the cliff and into the story armed with very little, and we hope for fair winds and kind thermals to help get us to the other side of the mountain range.

Bryce Courtenay used the metaphor of a train journey. He told me that some writers know exactly which station they're leaving from and where to alight to reach their final destination. They also know all the stops the train will make along the way. They know how long the journey will take, they've checked the weather, they've made sure the trains are running on time. They've packed carefully for the journey: they know exactly what gear they need to take with them for a successful and happy trip. Meanwhile my kin are hoping there's a train that might leave today. We're not especially fussed where it's going. It's going somewhere – that's all that matters to us. We have no idea where it'll stop, either. We're comfortable to go wherever the train takes us and we'll jump off when we find a place that appeals. We don't pack much, in fact we don't even need a suitcase. We grab a couple of essentials with the view that we'll buy what we need as we go.

That image he painted always made sense to me. And it reassured me because when I started out, I was sitting in a writing masterclass chock-full of planners. Not recognising at the time that we writers come in all shapes and sizes, particularly in terms of how we approach the craft, I immediately felt I was doing something wrong. His metaphor helped immensely.

Of course in between the planners and the freefallers are a host of writers who have qualities of the two: some plan a great deal but not all of the story, while others have a vague plan but take the gun-slinging approach to plotting it out. I'm convinced you don't choose. You arrive at writing with these qualities inbuilt. And I say this with conviction because I have tried, and failed, so many times to plan my story. I do intensive research but I don't ever really think about the plot itself, I know it will come when the time to write arrives. I'll talk more about research later.

From time to time I find myself envying the planners because they have lovely Moleskin notebooks brimming with information. The planners have always struck me as being more writerly.

Me, I have nothing. Nothing!

I have tried taking walks with the dog with the deliberate intention to consider future scenes. I put on my headphones, I set out vigorously with a determined frown. And within moments I'm thinking about what to cook for dinner, or Colin Firth climbing out of the lake as Mr Darcy or worse, I start daydreaming about a new story, or my next pair of winter boots, or whether Daniel Craig ever will consider being Colonel Kilian in the movie of *The Lavender Keeper* – if there ever is a movie of *The Lavender Keeper*. I think about whether to have my fringe cut thicker or what to do with those limes that are about to drop off our tree. I think about our sons, our family, the fact that our neighbour's son constantly steals the shade of the tree that we planted thirty years ago to give us shade to park beneath. I wonder who it is that regularly throws banana skins on the kerb as they ride their bike around the corner of our street. I wonder about global warming, war, and whether all this walking is helping my arthritis. My thoughts spin for the entire forty-five minutes I'm out pounding the pavement.

Needless to say, I think about everything but the manuscript I'm working on. And so, over the past decade of writing I've learned that planning doesn't work for me; it works for some but not for all of us.

There are disadvantages to both types.

Planners can potentially spend so much time in their plotting, their characters and the design of the book's architecture that they risk getting lost in the mire. These are often the people who admit to me that they've been 'working on a book for a few years.' What they mean is that they keep fiddling with the first few chapters they've written and don't progress and all the while they are busy researching, planning scenes, drawing graphs, pinning up characters references, doing pie charts, flow charts, Venn diagrams and calculating on slide rules. If you are extremely anal about plotting and planning the story, there is a very real danger of becoming your own worst enemy. Plunging into writing can be the hardest part.

There is nothing wrong in being a planner, let me add. But it helps to recognise how you're wired as a writer. If you sense you are a planner or bear some of a high-end planner's qualities, then the discipline of goal-setting is going to be extremely important for you. Sticking to a word-count equation, which I'll cover in more depth in the next chapter, will keep you focused and force you to confront the writing by leaving the planning stage.

Meanwhile the primary pothole awaiting freefallers is that lack of story direction means you can often write yourself into a corner. Then you have to either find the confidence to write yourself out of it or backtrack, trashing the previous few scenes because they haven't worked. The story will wander, characters will bob up, your writing will always feel ever so slightly out of control and as it races off down unknown tracks you might be unsure how to bring the story back to its original path. This is normal for a freefaller. It's the world I inhabit. I know that I will do my hardest yards later alongside an editor who will help me cut away all that meandering. And then there's the *damn it!* situation for those who write series, where, much later when you're in the midst of your second volume draft, you realise how much better the story could have been if only you'd planned properly for a particular event in the first volume. Sigh. I have faced this many times when writing fantasy trilogies.

On the bright side, freefallers tend to be the writers who get on and get finished far more easily. They don't fret along the way – well, not nearly as much as the planner who can be trapped by his or her original plan. (Remember Rimmer from *Red Dwarf*? He spends so much time organising his elaborate study plan that he can't get down to study. With each passing day he revises the plan until it's too late to sit the exam.) Freefallers give themselves freedom to explore hidden pathways to the story and that gives their tales an exciting whiff of unpredictability and it also opens up the story to possibilities. We aren't locked in by pre-set parameters in other words.

If you are fortunate enough to be both tarred by the planning squad and feathered by the freefalling gang, then you're in a prime position to deliver fast, very well-thought-out manuscripts. And I really do envy you.

To be fair, most writers sit somewhere near the centre. I'm just a raging freefaller and the twisty-turny nature of all my books, no matter which genre I'm writing, attests to that. Plus, I do admit that the storytelling is a personal pleasure because it's a mystery for me and I like the surprises of my own tales. For instance, I am currently writing a novel that I thought would be about the making of a grand perfume, in the heyday of perfume-making, using all natural products in the perfume capital of Grasse in southern Provence. But because I have no plan to my story, what has actually emerged is a tale of two powerful perfume families and a dark, sinful secret that binds them. I had no idea the secret was coming – it stole up and took control of the keyboard.

Either way, you are what you are and I suggest you don't fight it. Instead, embrace it. If you're a planner accept that it can be a real blessing to know where you're headed with the manuscript. But it's only a blessing if you are disciplined enough to sit behind the screen and get on with the writing that you've planned for. And freefallers can't help themselves – love who you are as a writer. You'll make other writers jealous by your speed and cavalier attitude – just make sure you don't get lost.

START DEVELOPING SOME GOOD HABITS FOR YOUR CAREER AS A WRITER

Successful writers tend to be creatures of habit. We don't all operate within the same structure, because everyone is wired differently, but each of us will follow certain rituals that work for us. It's wise to develop some good habits to ensure that you get to your writing regularly, maintain your output and stay bright and healthy through the process.

Finding your ideal routine

Work out a routine that respects your lifestyle and that of your family and allows you to sit in front of your computer daily for a period of uninterrupted time. Because we're all different, our routines will vary wildly. Some people can allow many hours to themselves, others perhaps only one per day. All that matters is what works for you. This is not a contest and no one is going to compare one routine to another, so you are not required to conform to any shape in terms of how and when you write. There are no rules. Don't worry about what anyone else is doing; worry only about what you can do and the time you can give to your writing.

If the only time of the day that you can spare is between 4 a.m. and 5 a.m. and you don't mind getting up early, then great. If you're a night owl and find it easy to work into the early hours – and you can spare two or three or just get less sleep – fabulous! If you can only find time in your lunch hour in the staff room or perhaps a few hours each afternoon at your local library, then that's what you have to work with.

There are writers who can work anywhere at any time. I can't. Despite my freefalling approach to the content of my writing, I have a need for routine. I prefer to be in the same place, same time, daily. That said, with the pressure of a deadline, I have been known to write from a cruise ship balcony and surprised myself with some of the best writing I've done.

Most of us who make a living from writing will admit

that a familiar space – our own desktops and quiet atmosphere – makes for a happy writing session. And as you flesh out your own routine, in turn the routine itself will help you achieve the discipline to finish your first novel.

Start by sorting out how much time you can give to your writing daily. Be conservative, don't stretch yourself so you are going to feel stressed and run the risk of wearing yourself out. If you have a job to hold down, a family to provide and care for or both, then it's important that your writing works around the day job and your family life – not the other way around.

When you know how much time you can give – let's say two hours as an example – then work out when you are going to give this time. Will it be the beginning, middle or end of the day?

Once you have nutted out these two fundamental questions, commit to your chosen period of time and time of the day and *stick to it*. Imagine it being chiselled into stone. This is a covenant you're making with yourself and it mustn't be broken.

Setting up a workable routine empowers you to write. Then you no longer have any excuses!

The D word that dominates my writing life: discipline

I really cannot stress the D word enough. You know how I mentioned that magical ingredient earlier? Well, this is it. This is the antithesis of being a dabbler, babbler or scribbler.

Discipline is what the successful commercial novelist

draws on to do the hard yards and hit her deadline. It's why a manuscript progresses each day. You have to find it in your writing life, embrace it and love it. It really is your best friend.

Without discipline, you'll make it much harder for yourself to become a successful commercial writer who can earn a living from books.

From discipline you'll find the energy you didn't know you had.

Discipline is when you walk away from the TV program that everyone else is watching or talking about. It's about having the ability to shut yourself off from social media – arguably the most insidious of distractions and a genuine threat to your writing. It's the capacity to make a phone call to a friend and limit it to the fifteen minutes you promised. It's when you say no to that night out with the gang because your writing schedule was thrown that day and you haven't written a thing.

This is the point at which you never give yourself an excuse to feel too weary, too full of a cold or sore throat, too over it, too underwhelmed or perhaps overwhelmed by the notion of writing the novel.

No one can give you this special quality, unfortunately. Discipline comes from within; we all possess it, we simply have to find it. It's how anyone with any goal achieves what they have set out to do, whether they're an athlete, student, or someone taking up a new hobby or skill. Discipline is arguably at the root of all success in any chosen venture and it is your very special friend for writing.

I can remember when my sons were in Year 11 and they decided that they'd share a lawn-mowing round. They liked the idea of working together and while I wouldn't call them the outdoorsy types, they were both into having their own small business and they had shared a lawnmower fascination since they were tiny tots.

My husband and I felt sure that the enchantment would wear thin as soon as it became their daily work but they seemed motivated and I'm all about motivation, enjoying one's work and doing what you want for a career rather than fitting someone else's vision of what you should do.

Anyway, while I privately blame *Boston Legal* and *Gray's Anatomy*, by the end of Year 11, one had decided he was going to pursue Law, the other became determined to find his way into Medicine. As parents, to say we were gobsmacked is an understatement. We had a long chat to both and I noted each had a shiny look of determination in his eyes. I sensed that they meant what they said – they intended to study Law and Medicine at university – but I needed to win a genuine commitment.

And so we had the Discipline Chat.

The boys and I drew up a contract – I may have even made them sign it – that held their studies to account. If they wanted my and Ian's help, we would support them every step of the way. We would pay for whatever the boys needed, we would keep the chores to the bare minimum and we would be their first readers and proofers. We would be the idiots who risked speeding fines to get assignments in on time and we would function as a taxi service wherever and whenever they needed us – but they had to be disciplined with their studies.

That discipline began with no television except for on Friday evenings.

No parties outside of school holidays.

They were to study every evening during the term and throughout the holidays if assignments were due or if they were lagging in revision.

They were not to miss an hour of Year 12 – we would give them no quarter for being tired.

They were to exercise daily.

We soon realised they were both working well into the wee hours every day, so the final stipulation was that they ate healthily and took vitamins to keep their strength up.

They committed. They got disciplined and I was the slave driver. I cracked that whip and we had a massive Year 12 together.

Neither of our sons is a born scholar. They both learned the reward that hard work, discipline and total commitment bring.

One is now in his Masters and PhD in paediatric neuropsychology. The other is about to finish the five-year slog of a double degree in Law and Business.

They are both hugely ambitious now and fully understand the discipline and commitment demanded of working towards a single goal.

Writing your novel is no different to committing to Year 12, to marriage, to being a champion athlete, to being the best you can be at anything from knitting to parenting.

And discipline is the packhorse that will bravely carry you for the whole journey.

The psychology of writing is deeply intriguing because we all have our quirks, our odd little routines. Our routines are good, they keep us on track and motivated. Some people won't leave their screens until a chapter is finished, for other people it's about time behind the screen: for instance, their discipline might be two hours per day.

My major driving discipline is my word count. I'll show you how I formulate my daily word-count equation, as it could help you too.

To illustrate why the goal of a word count works for me I should explain that I am weirdly motivated by numbers. I add up oddities like passport numbers, number plates, hotel rooms, flight details, telephone numbers, registration details, credit card numbers, the list is endless. I know, it's crazy, right? But if I can wrestle them into a number I like – let's not go there – then I feel comforted. Now my poor husband has to check whether I like a stateroom number on a cruise ship before he books us in, just so I don't have to feel confronted. I've taught myself how to push through when a number I don't like enters my life – I can't always do much about it without appearing to be a total loony – but if I can avoid feeling uncomfortable I do. My publicist and I now check hotel room numbers when the keys are handed over at reception and I get first choice based on the number.

When I'm writing, as soon as I hit my daily word count, it doesn't matter whether I'm at the end of a chapter or in the middle of a sentence, I stop. I don't feel guilty, anxious or obliged to complete the sentence, either. The next day I usually frown and wonder where I was going with that thought but given that this is how I operate, I don't let it trouble me.

What I want you to do is not let what others do trouble you. Again I repeat, we are all different and we all come to writing in different ways. I know people who believe in writer's block. I don't subscribe to it. Meanwhile, the first thing I want to do after a writing session is to go for some exercise and others want a glass of wine or a cup of coffee and some down time. I don't talk about my story while I'm writing it – that's probably because I don't know what's going to happen in it – but I know others who enjoy discussing their projects. We're all different, you see, so don't be derailed by others. Just because I can be across several writing projects a year, it doesn't mean you need to be. That's me, I'm wired differently. You can probably do all sorts of amazing stuff that I can't but I don't let that trouble me. I just focus on what I can do – because secretly that's all I care about.

One final point on the psychology of writers. I will never tackle a writing project if I don't think I can be a winner at it. I know that sounds horribly arrogant but

I don't see it that way. I see it as honest. I'm being true to myself in admitting this. I only write when I believe I can deliver a good story that people will want to read: so fantasy fiction came naturally, a crime thriller felt comfy to handle once I'd gained my confidence in fantasy and sweeping historical adventures with romantic settings felt completely natural. Whenever I set out to write a story, even though I don't know the plot, I feel confident in my storytelling. I know that I've chosen the right genre to deliver an engaging read that fits the popular fiction brand.

I'll admit there are genres that I'd love to have a go at – for instance, women's fiction in a contemporary setting is speaking loudly to me but until I feel assured that I can deliver a ripping story set in today's world, I won't attempt one.

When I know my strengths and I play to them, there are no excuses for not finishing.

Exercise

Time away from the keyboard is as important as disciplined writing time. Get into a good exercise routine. Being hunched over a computer isn't healthy for anyone. Stretch each hour – this can be achieved simply by getting up and walking around the garden, office, whatever. Wave your arms around and open up those shoulders.

Take a long walk every day. Writers spend a lot of time indoors, so we need our Vitamin D and fresh air. Walk briskly, don't amble. Exercise has a happy knack of blowing out the cobwebs in your mind. That scene you've been struggling with, that character you're not quite sure about, or a subplot that you know you need but aren't ready to leap into? It will slot into place in a far more breezy fashion if you keep up a good exercise routine. Curiously, the storytelling aspect seems to happen because you're not thinking about it.

In fact, don't think about anything. Just let your mind drift while you walk. This is the time that the artist in you will start to notice cloud formations, how trees look, how people move and so on. Don't force it though. If you force it, you might feel a bit daft and the craft of your writing a little contrived. Just open up your mind to random thoughts, let the images arrive and slot into the memory bank for future use.

I'm a great believer in the back of the brain taking care of business in its own mysterious way. When I'm exercising, as I've told you already, I'm rarely, if ever, focusing on my stories but I do believe my imagination is busy at its job without me realising it because I'm relaxed and distracted.

If you're a gym junkie or a dance enthusiast, great! Any form of exercise is terrific and it doesn't have to cost you a cent. Just walk out of your front gate and keep going in a big circle.

You will feel healthier for the effort and your storytelling will benefit infinitely.

Sleep

Acting as a good counterbalance to regular exercise is a good sleep pattern. Get into one if you can. Try not to go to bed at all hours. I'm a night owl so I tend to go to bed at midnight or beyond, but I do that every night so my body's used to it. I don't go to bed at 9 p.m. one night and then hit the pillow at 2 a.m. the next. Everyone's needs are different. I function on six hours' sleep quite happily. Seven or eight would be marvellous if I could achieve that but I can't. Some of you may need eight or even nine hours. Just make sure that you have quality sleeping time when you get to bed. I firmly believe that all my best plotting is done while I sleep and dream.

And yes, I have battled through the restlessness of menopause, onset of arthritis and the realisation that caffeine after 6 p.m. is not my friend, and that physical exhaustion doesn't necessarily equate to mental fatigue. But I don't make excuses, I just make sure I am in bed for six hours at least and can blame no one but myself if I don't get a good kip. Some of us can't. My calf cramps can wake the entire neighbourhood but I still get up and make my word contract the next day. Do the best you can with the time available to you.

Light

Well, I don't want to get all boffinish on you but the circadian rhythm shouldn't be ignored. Our internal clocks help us maintain a healthy existence. If you have chickens, for instance, as we do, you'll know how they head to the coop as the light falls. Our circadian rhythm ticks away too and motivates us to rise and to sleep and it adjusts according to the season and conditions around us. The most important condition is light.

I'll never forget my joy when I was able to take off one day a week from our business to commit to my writing. It was a Friday. And it was better than jewellery, a new pair of winter boots or even chocolate! For years I had written at night – I produced my first five novels working in the dark hours and never thought much about it until I had this glittering Friday each week and suddenly I was writing by daylight. Wow! It made me realise that light is vital, not just to see better by but to feel brighter – I know that that sounds obvious but sometimes we don't grasp the obvious until it slams into us, just like my Friday writing day did. Even if you do have to write at night, please make sure the light you're working by is bright and plentiful. Don't fatigue your eyes unnecessarily and try some daylight writing as soon as possible.

Technology and Resources

Make sure you have a proper chair, suitable for typing. Ensure that it is at the correct height and that it's ergonomically sound. Writers suffer all sorts of injuries from being at the keyboard for so many hours, so limit the damage: keep your chair at the right height, have a workable desk and a good keyboard and try if you can to maintain good posture. Stretch regularly: loosen up those shoulders by rolling them, cross and uncross your legs and move your neck about.

Update your computer equipment as often as you can afford to. Don't keep working on an old bomb that might fail on you, or simply not handle the work or programs you need it to. I know computer technology is constantly progressing and it's frustrating that today's hot item is tomorrow's dinosaur but keep up as best you can. Buy the best quality you can afford, it'll save you from needing to update so frequently. I upgrade my computer every couple of years and I work with a desktop computer for the daily grind but I also find a laptop is a great asset. Because the only tool I need for my work is a computer, I have invested in an iMac desktop along with a MacBook Air to take with me when I travel and research.

That said, all I needed to write my first five books was a single computer. I came from a magazine publishing background so we had been using Mac computers since they were invented. Very good computer equipment was part of my daily landscape and so I just swapped the desktop I used for our business to the desktop I used for my writing. But I did begin to invest in computers, for instance I upgraded to a large screen, specifically for my work, once I was making a living from my writing. It's a relatively small investment given that it's the tool that encapsulates my whole world: it's how I earn my money, how I communicate with colleagues, friends and family, and how I run the business of novels.

If you're just starting out with your first novel manuscript, you don't need all the paraphernalia on offer – just ensure you have access to a reliable computer and keep in mind that the single most important aspect of your computer technology is data storage. Get professional advice on how to back up your precious work. I have my ideas on what equipment is best but you need to sort out what suits your needs and budget. But please, make sure that you have external back-up storage for your work, be it on a hard drive or in the cloud, it doesn't matter. And please, please, please – *back up your work daily*.

Be disciplined about it, it will save your bacon one day.

You don't need tailored programs for producing manuscripts although I've played with one of the better ones – Scrivener – and really enjoyed it. That said, I've happily produced all of my novels using Microsoft Word for Mac and no other fancy bits and pieces, just the data storage whirring quietly away in the background and a USB for the evening's physical back-up. I wear the USB on a lanyard and if someone yelled 'Fire!' that's the first thing I'd grab, along with the family, dogs, chooks and bake ware. I put it on in the morning and I take it off and leave it by the bedside at night. Again, this is simply a routine and part of the discipline.

Outside of the aforementioned computer and suitable writing chair and desk, you really need little more than internet access and a quiet space. Everything else is a bonus.

While I do love my huge dictionary and thesaurus and they're always handy to have nearby, the online resources are so fast and brilliant these days that even these wonderful books are sadly starting to gather dust.

I wrote my first few books from my imagination but these days I have a swag of research material that I plough through and it's mostly books. Nonfiction books are a resource I now can't live without and each novel requires I tackle a different tower of reading material. I order books from all over the world for research, they always feel more enriching, powerful and intimate than Google.

Google is brilliant but writing entirely from Wikipedia, for instance, keeps your research at a relatively shallow, generalised level. Someone writing historical fiction needs to get deep into the era and specific books on specific subjects can't be underestimated for their powerful ability to breathe oxygen in and around your story.

Avoid being a one-trick pony

Have other interests. It's healthy and it stops you from thinking, talking and even boring others with your novel.

Writing is happily all-consuming. You can get lost in your story and while being absorbed is healthy, you don't want the book to become all that you think about.

Nor do I think that letting the writing of the novel define you is wise. Let your writing be one of your interests. Adopting this less stringent mindset will empower you not to get too self-absorbed or obsessed by the book. People who only talk about their manuscripts are thoroughly dull. People who talk about writing too much are just as yawn-inspiring.

You do need down time and the best way to achieve that is to have some sort of small hobby. Besides, it's good for your wellbeing to have other pastimes.

Now, I know that fitting a hobby into a life that is already crammed full may feel like overload, right? You're earning a living, raising a family perhaps, being a good partner, exercising, sleeping well, remembering posture *and* writing a book. But having an enjoyable distraction from writing – one that's not work- or household-chore related – is very good for your writing and for your health. I'm not talking about taking up something huge and daunting. It may be something as simple as learning how to knit, setting up a herb patch, taking a pottery course or going to the movies once a week. For me it's baking.

Baking once terrified me but in my mid forties I decided I was going to beat this monster. Since turning fifty baking has become my pleasurable hobby away from writing. I love to cook but I love to bake most of all. It's creative, a challenge and absorbing, it distracts me brilliantly, I can share it with my family and friends, and I have something to show for my toil at the end of it. I love it. Whenever I'm baking, I'm away in a quiet world, not really thinking about anything much and definitely not thinking about books. I like knowing that while I'm fiddling around with pastries and cakes, measuring and stirring, mixing and tasting, my back of brain is taking care of business – just as it does when I exercise and sleep – and working out the next step of my latest novel's plot.

Having a hobby isn't a must but writing is a very lonely task; it can't be shared with anyone and it is utterly selfish and can alienate others. You have to remove yourself, be quiet and alone, and that can be hard, especially on those you are closest to. A hobby is a way of reconnecting and dragging you off the desert island that writing puts you on. If you can find a pastime that lets you enjoy it alongside partners, friends, family, then it's a valuable addition to your life.

My editor wondered whether travel is my hobby. It's a good question because I do cover a lot of geography most years. I began travelling very young, I was under five when I went on my first journey with my parents, and in my late teens I struck out alone. Then I joined the travel industry and travelled constantly for a couple of decades. All of those extensive travel experiences that I thought I'd forgotten about now inform my writing, which I'm enormously grateful for. Anyone reading this who travels is in a fortunate position for all the same reasons.

My travels have given and continue to give me a rich resource and palette from which to paint my stories. And now, curiously, I'm travelling more than ever. These days it's with specific research for my books in mind. Learning about different countries' histories and culture is vital to my storytelling. Even so, travel has always been about work for me. I rarely, if ever, go on holiday. My last real holiday was for four days in the year 2010. In this instance I was forced into it because I didn't want to celebrate my fiftieth on home soil – I loathe parties and so I ran away.

I can't remember the last time I properly holidayed, to be honest. Maybe it was twenty years ago when our children were very young. I'm not a person who sits still for very long anyway – only a book, movie or flight can keep me in one spot for a protracted period.

Travel for me always has been and, I suspect, always will be a necessity. I realise that most people would love to have that necessity in their life but when others are sipping a wine at a street-side café or luxuriating in a resort, I'm probably in the bowels of a museum or library somewhere trawling for information. I'm rarely the person on the open-topped bus or giggling in front of the camera at some iconic spot without a care in the world. There's always a reason that I am anywhere in the world – be it for a book or an article. Travelling and writing is wonderful work if you can get it but it is still work with a deadline and piece of writing due at the end of it.

So no, travel is not a hobby – I travel for work but it's fun, rewarding and enriching.

Distance

Time away from your manuscript is healthy. I subscribe to writing daily but I also take the weekend off. And when you've finished the initial draft it is a worthwhile practice to put that story away for a while. Resist the urge to touch it, edit it, read it, even skim it. Just leave it alone. If you can leave it for at least six weeks you'll be doing yourself a favour. Come back to it and you'll read it with a genuinely fresh pair of eyes – trust me on this – and you'll be surprised not only that you really did finish a whopping novel but you'll have the benefit of distance. You'll be more critical, more prepared to edit and trim, more comfortable about constructive changes.

3.

GETTING STARTED

You've told the people closest to you that you are determined to settle down and write your novel. You've got their support and they want to see you succeed at this project, so they will do their best to give you the space and time you need because you are going to be extremely reasonable about how often and how long you withdraw from them. Right? Good.

What else do you need?

QUIET SPACE – THIS IS YOUR MOST IMPORTANT ASSET BEYOND YOUR IMAGINATION

Writing is a lonely task. No one can help you do the work. Company is irritating. Interruptions are frustrating; even someone offering you a kindly cup of tea at the wrong moment can throw off your train of thought. But let's not get too precious about it. What is desirable is a tiny area to put your computer on some sort of desk with a chair – apart from a fabulous sunlit loft with huge picture windows and walls lined with books and your own coffee machine, as well as an endless supply of chocolate and super-duper fast internet, that is.

I began at the kitchen table but worked when everyone was asleep so it was just the dogs and me. All was quiet.

When it seemed this 'books thing' as my husband used to call it was going to take off, we cleared out an upstairs cubby and I worked from there. I stared at a blank wall. When the book contracts began to flow he converted our garden shed into a small writing cottage. Leaves would blow in, the dogs could bash their way in because the door was dodgy and spiders were unhappy companions for me but I loved that I was working away from the house. I could hear the washing machine whirr and thump away nearby and I got as used to its sounds as a growing child in its mother's womb is comforted by her mother's heartbeat. I recently moved again. Ian wanted to turn 'the writing cottage' into a garage. Our sons had grown up and have cars of their own now: we needed the off-street parking so as not annoy the young neighbours who, as you may recall, are stealing the shade we set up thirty years ago.

Anyway, I was transported back indoors and upstairs to where I'd sat a dozen years previous – identical spot – except this time Ian had put in a new dividing wall and air conditioning, added a huge picture window because he knows my need for light, and a door because he also knows my desire to lock myself away. The space is tiny with no bookshelves or clutter – it's just me, my desk, a framed head shot of Bryce Courtenay grinning at me and reminding me of promises I gave him about my writing and a large Buzz Lightyear figurine who talks, which I was given for a birthday a decade ago because he so inspired me. I look out over the rooftops of our neighbourhood and I am warm in winter, cool in summer and, above all, alone and so happy as I write. For someone already past her thirtieth novel, this is quite an ordinary little space with few trappings but it has everything I need.

We recently made the enormous decision to ditch city life in favour of an escapist country lifestyle living on the fringe of one of the wine districts in Australia. We've found an old stone farmhouse in desperate need of renovation. It has a cluster of stone outbuildings and eight acres with roses and potting sheds, vegetable gardens and even a chook shed. It's perfect. I would be happy to write in the chook shed with my feathered friends clucking around me but this books thing of mine deserves some respect according to my husband and so an old barn is to be converted into a studio. I'm excited, obviously, but the truth is, I'm workmanlike about what I do and I don't get caught up in the romance of being a writer – I discovered early the hard yards of the journey of any book. So long as

I have the essentials, the book will happen.

I remember when I spent a year writing from my pantry! I know, it's bizarre. But there were a couple of reasons for the shift there. We were renovating and I quickly wearied of the parade of tradies who passed my shed in the garden, staring in every time they walked by. I mean, it happened dozens of times a day. They'd wave, they'd call out things like 'How's your brochure thing going?' they'd grin, they'd step inside and say 'Sorry to disturb you, but we were just wondering where the garden tap is?' or, my particular favourite, they'd take phone calls directly outside my window. Tradies are mostly deaf I'm sure because they talk very loudly into their mobile phones that go off all day long. During that time I'd grit my teeth as I was forced to share everything with them, from their plumbing equipment orders through to arguments with their partner. I killed many husbands and wives in my stories as a sort of silent revenge for the interruptions.

Disruptive renovations and my passion for cooking worked in concert to usher me into my new space – a big pantry – surrounded by food, my baking gear, my beloved coffee machine and in close proximity to my stashes of chocolate hidden from my sons. It may strike the rest of the world as odd but frankly, it was my favourite ever writing spot. It was such a light and friendly space and I was left alone because no one could see me. Perfect!

The conclusion to this is that if you can fit a small table and chair in the cubby under the stairs, it's better than being in the family room where all the living gets done. If you live alone, you don't have this problem but I would still advise you set up a dedicated working space so you can instantly focus when you sit down in that area.

The aim of your own tiny spot is that everyone knows about it. It's from here that you're going to write your novel and you need to be left alone to do it.

SET UP YOUR WORKING PARAMETERS

Setting up your working parameters is important. How much time can you give each day or how many words are you aiming to write each session?

One hour is fine, by the way, even half an hour is fine. Set your goal and stick to it – whether it's a number of words, a period of time spent writing, a scene per session, a chapter per week, whatever.

I've mentioned that I use a writing equation of my own design. For me it's all about how many words I write per day.

This may not work for you but it works a charm for me. I am horrible at maths but as I explained earlier, I have a bit of an OCD thing for numbers. I count when I brush my teeth for goodness sake. My family now knows not to interrupt me when brushing or I have to start again! Having this word-count equation makes me feel comfortable. What's more, it is the most incredibly motivating driver in my writing life. I live by this equation because the numbers never lie.

Whenever I put my equation up on a whiteboard or explain it to a roomful of writers, I can usually hear a pin drop when I finish. It makes a lot of sense to new writers, especially those who are feeling overwhelmed by the enormity of tackling a novel. The thought of having to put together 120 000 words while ensuring great storytelling, brisk pace, fabulous characterisations, crisp dialogue and credible situations is daunting.

I understand all of this because I was a new writer not so long ago, and I designed my equation when I was starting out. It's my special 'thing', it's a comfort blanket that gives me my whole sense of security while I'm writing. If I stick to the equation the book will take care of itself.

So, here it is, see how you go with it.

Planners will love it! Hopefully freefallers will be delighted at the sense of security it gives them, even when their storytelling remains entirely out of control.

Bryce Courtenay was certainly appalled that I hadn't shared this with him earlier than 2012.

Let's build your equation.

The word-count equation
Step 1
Which popular fiction genre does your manuscript fit best?

Knowing your genre will help guide you with an estimated word count. Your book can be as long as you want it to be but certain lines of logic can direct your decision. For example, a 600-page book looks daunting for the reader.

To ensure that the book doesn't get too weighty, the publisher may decide to typeset the text very tightly, resulting in a small font that's difficult to read.

Of course in these days of ebooks that's not such an issue but I'm still proceeding with the notion that you want a traditional book – even if it is something that you print on demand or print down the track after ebook success.

What's more, if you're thinking of the global market for your book, consider the translation costs – they are *huge*. The more words you have, the higher the cost and the less appealing it is for that foreign publisher to purchase the rights.

Here is a rough guide to word counts broken down by genre:

- Historical: 110 000
- Fantasy: 130 000
- Sci-Fi: 100 000
- Crime: 90 000
- Romance: 100 000
- Chicklit: 85 000
- Horror: 90 000
- Young Adult: 80 000

A novel is a fluid beast, so the decision is guesswork and you can add or subtract another 10 000 or so words to these estimations. A happy medium is roughly 100 000 words for any popular fiction novel.

Remember this too: be prepared to see your words

pared back. The editorial process can trim anything from sentences to whole chapters.

But for the sake of the equation, you need to pick a number that looks right for the genre, so let's work with 100 000 as a starting point.

Step 2

What is your starting date? Write it down!

For the purposes of this exercise let's say 1 January.

Step 3

When is your deadline? Set yourself a reasonable time frame within which to finish your novel. I'm presuming you're reading this because you are just setting out on your writing adventure, so I recommend giving yourself twelve months and factor in a generous eight weeks off throughout that time to account for holidays and sick days.

So, 31 December it is. Happy with that?

Good.

Now you are working with forty-four weeks, which is more than enough to give you a slow, steady, entirely un-panicked period of time in which to produce the first draft of your novel.

Step 4

Now decide how many days in that week you are going to commit to writing. No, *not* seven, that's unrealistic. Even six days per week is not wise.

In case this helps you, I see four days per week as fundamental. Sometimes I'll write five. When I'm travelling, which is often, I don't write any days per week. When I'm working from Tasmania, a place I think of as my haven, I write six days per week. It doesn't matter how you portion it up, you need to commit to a certain number of writing days each week.

Shall we say four, as I do?

Step 5

All right, now it's coming together. For the sake of this equation, you are committing to write your manuscript as follows:

Four days per week for forty-four weeks of the year.

That gives you 176 working days in total.

And you've committed to writing a novel that is 100 000 words long. Agreed?

Step 6

Now divide 100 000 by 176 and the magic number of 568 appears. Oh, blimey, I love that number! And if you like that trilogy of numerals stick with it, or feel free to round it up to 600.

Step 7

You're there, you have your equation so write it down.

You are going to write 568 words per session. Yes?

Yes!

This is your milestone figure. You hold yourself to this number every day, it is the contract you make with yourself. If you write more, well done but don't include it in tomorrow's words.

Only today matters. Yesterday's words are in the vault. Tomorrow's words are coming.

There is no need to write more than 600 words daily but you must not allow yourself to write fewer than 568 words per day.

This is your personal equation for this particular novel.

I generate a different equation for each novel, depending on my time availability, what I'm writing, how much research is required, what the deadline for delivery is and so on. But the equation itself keeps me focused, keeps me pushing forwards to the goal, keeps the words moving. With it, I know that I will always finish the novel by the deadline set.

And here's the beautiful thing about the equation. If you begin on 1 January and write 568 words each day, for four days each week, for forty-four weeks of the year, then you will have a finished draft of your novel by 31 December.

The numbers always deliver, so long as you remain disciplined and stick to your contract.

You need never think of yourself as a dabbler again!

There is a Step 8, but only do it if you're as much of an oddball as I am.

Step 8

Invest in a huge calculator. The bigger the better. Go for the one that sparkles, is fluorescent or has huge fake jewels. I used to have one that was almost the size of my printer and using it gave me great delight. Anything jumbo-sized is always a piece of comedy.

On your calculator, you can tot up how you're going with overall word count. If the writing is slow going, the need to keep checking your sufficiently increasing tally will drive you. If it's happening fast, realising how many words you've already written will bring you a whoop of pleasure.

I have one that has a comical beep attached to each digit. My family can hear it beep from all over the house. They know when it's beeping hysterically that the writing is harder going because I'm obviously checking progress often. Other times they hear it only once, maybe twice in a session and I'm back among the family swiftly, smiling benignly because my writing is done for the day.

Stop when you reach your agreed contract. No need to write on (I've told you I often stop mid sentence). If you do, that's your choice but today's additional words do not come off tomorrow's tally.

Every day is groundhog day. You start again and that's how books get written fast, without you losing rhythm and to deadline.

This is a typical equation of mine and I update it every day so I always know where I am in the manuscript:

-   Start date: 19 June

- Deadline date: 29 November
- Actual working period: 20 weeks
- Working days: 80 days
- Target words: 120 000
- Daily target: 1500
- Yesterday's total: 2605
- Today's total: 2789
- Actual completion date: Completed 30 September in 70 working days
- TOTAL: 127 578
- Words to go: None

Sometimes I'll add my rolling weekly word count totals to this tally, just to keep me on my toes and my calculator whirring.

The upshot of all these numbers is that not only do I have a magic figure to reach but I keep a running total of yesterday's word count, how many words I've written in total and how many words I've got to go based on that magic total of 120 000 word contract.

I don't do this because I'm a loony, I do it to keep myself motivated. Looking at those figures each day drives me. Tapping crazily on my calculator helps me to stay in motion. The accumulation of words will always push the story forwards.

And it may work for you too.

I shared this process with Bryce Courtenay at his final

masterclass in Canberra, just weeks before he passed away in 2012. He stared at me speechless, almost cross. 'Bloody hell, you could have saved me years if you'd shared that earlier,' he admonished. After that he first urged me to agree to take on his legacy of guiding new writers via a masterclass and then he insisted I put my experience and processes – like the writing equation – into a book for aspiring writers. The early draft excited him and he was especially delighted by its no-nonsense, practical attitude.

Anyway, go on, see if the writing equation works for you.

SET UP YOUR WORKING DOCUMENT

How you work with your draft manuscript comes down to personal preference.

I had always worked with one single document for my novel until I road-tested working in chapters with my most recently published book. Working in small sections makes it easy to navigate the document you're focussing on at the time. However, when I wanted to look back and check something I'd written – the spelling of a name, the colour of someone's eyes – then it became clumsy. It's trial and error to sort out what works best for you.

Since the last experience, I have returned to working from one large document.

I have road-tested the Scrivener writing software. I think it's terrific but I don't believe I'm the sort of writer it was produced for. I don't tend to use lots of notes or digital documents as reference material. I've tried glossaries and they are valuable but I'm useless at referring to them. I've also tried working with a timeline document, which is brilliant but you have to be willing to update it whenever you fiddle with the dates and seasons in your story. (I constantly play with dates and seasons, I'll admit.)

Scrivener is superb for keeping a constant reference on characters, research, ideas and notes to self about aspects of the manuscript you must attend to.

But I am a diehard, gun-slinging sort of writer who cannot plan a sentence or scene, let alone attend to a glossary or pinboard. I just don't work that way.

If you're an intense planner with loads of reference material that you want to refer to constantly, then one of these writing programs such as Scrivener may suit you brilliantly.

I would encourage you to be organised.

Here's a general yardstick for your main document:
- Leader page: working title, your name, your contact details, a word count and submission date.
- General header: working title of the novel, your name and phone number.
- Footer: page number on the right-hand side.
- Font: Times Roman is easy to read – serif fonts lead the eye to the next word, improving readability. Don't be tempted to use fancy fonts: you'll look amateurish for starters and you'll quickly tire the eyes of the agent and commissioning editor.

- Spacing: double-lined spacing for easy reading and mark-up.
- Margins: a minimum 3.5 cm margin on either side is ideal for editorial mark-up.
- Delivery: today's commissioning editors will likely ask you to submit a digital version of your manuscript in a Word doc file of 2MB or less. Ensure that you follow the submissions guidelines on the individual publisher's website.
- If you've been asked for a printed copy of the manuscript, which today seems unlikely, never be tempted to use staples. Don't use graphics or cutesy pictures on your submission either, and don't include quotes or testimonials, unless they've been specifically requested by the commissioning editor.
- And please do not submit your cover design. I get asked this question regularly by new writers who have a friend who is an artist with great ideas for the cover. Major publishers – like mine, Penguin Random House – do not need you to submit cover art. Keep in mind that your submission of your draft manuscript for consideration by a publisher is a long way from a contract offer. And in turn a contract offer is a long way from cover design.
- There are whole teams at the publisher committed to artwork, and the aspects that come into play are wide and varied. A minty green, for instance, curiously pervaded the background hue of a

number of commercial fiction blockbusters over
the past Christmas bookselling period. But even
those types of coincidental oddities aside, the sales
team will have a great deal to say about what should
be on the cover, as will marketing and publicity, as
will your editorial team who will play with the actual
subject that the cover might focus on. The cover is
more about branding than it is about the book itself
although obviously it can't divorce itself entirely
from the story. The cover will always echo the
story but it's essentially about setting up the right
atmosphere for your storytelling and about getting
a 'look' right that speaks about you as a writer. It's
complex, often contrary, expensive, emotional and
best you stay out of it until asked. Your opinion
and ideas will be valued but you should not
physically submit designs. And your ideas only
become relevant when you have a contract and
the publishing team is at the point of planning a
cover – not a moment before.

Avoid loading up your submission with any of the 'noise'
I've referred to in this section. If you're trying to get your
manuscript noticed, make sure it's not for the wrong
reasons. The noise will not be appreciated by literary
agents, your gateway into the publishing world, nor by
the commissioning editor within the publishing house, if
you are submitting directly.

The creed is to keep your document plain and user friendly. Ensure lots of white space around the words – in the margins and between lines. Set up the document according to the wishes of the agent or the publisher that you are targeting. Start by reading the submission guidelines on the literary agent's and publisher's websites. For further formatting tips specific to writing fiction, it pays to visit the website of your local writers' centre.

GLOSSARY

I am not very good at planning. Actually that's a lie. I'm a compulsive list-maker in daily life but when it comes to my books, I'm useless at planning ahead, as I've explained. I wish I did make a glossary as I set out with each new novel because it would save a lot of time searching for stuff later.

So don't do as I do, do as I say. Take some wise advice given to me by Megan Lindholm aka Robin Hobb – one of the world's most successful writers before writing software was developed – and keep a simple reference glossary on your desktop.

Into this glossary you can sling titbits of helpful information relating to your book. You might reference each character including brief rundown of their physical features, personality quirks and other relevant background data. Keep it brief!

You can add place names to the glossary if you're writing a fantasy, clues if you're writing a thriller or dates if you're writing historical fiction. I recommend throwing in a timeline too, which you will thank me for down the track. Set out as you mean to go on. This is all part of getting disciplined and professional in your work. Timelines, incidentally, are where the manuscript often gets out of control for me. I'm sure a lot of my days have fifty-two hours in them for all the action that my characters indulge in.

A glossary is the place to record what time of year it is in your manuscript. Don't just list that it's winter, for instance, but identify that if it's midwinter then the nights are at their longest and roads may be covered with ice that wasn't there at the start of the season.

Let's say your book has moved along a few months. Now you can check back to your glossary when the story began and know that your action is playing out at the end of spring.

The glossary should be a simple, user friendly, easy-to-access reference. Don't cram it or it will become just another cumbersome file of information.

BOOK FOLDER

Now put your main document/s, your working glossary your word-count equation and all other files relevant to the novel into a dedicated folder on your desktop. Title it by the name of the novel.

File everything connected with the book into this folder including items of interest, photos and thoughts.

BACKING UP

I'm sure you know the frustration of losing work electronically. It can happen because of a glitch, an accidental deletion or the simple fact that you forgot to save your work. It happens. But you can minimise the damage by getting yourself into the habit of saving the document manually every few minutes.

I know this sounds a bit manic but it's now second nature for me to save every time I finish writing a paragraph. It's not time consuming, it's not even cumbersome; to be honest I barely register myself doing it any more. While my computer's automatic back-up is reliable I don't believe it's infallible as my screen has frozen frustratingly and I have now learned to take control of saving my work by doing it myself – manually and then via a separate external drive that is whirring away behind my computer 24-hours daily, and then onto the USB I spoke of that I leave bedside. It's pedantic but if it saves my life just once it has to be worth the tiny extra trouble. Incidentally, I have excellent equipment and still my iMac freezes now and then for inexplicable reasons, especially when Track Changes is on and manipulating a vast 700-page document.

The rule here is to *back up after every writing session.*

Take the precaution and back up with the same routine approach that you brush your teeth.

And don't lend that flash drive to anyone.

WRITER WRITING

Take your work seriously and be professional about it.

Jealously guard that time you've given yourself to write with the same fiery approach that a new mother has when she's finally got her baby to sleep.

Feel free to hang a sign on your front door that says 'Writer writing. Please do not disturb'.

For many who are juggling a job with their writing – as I did for the first five years – there should be no guilt in being inflexible with that time you've committed for writing. People at your workplace will think you're having a day off of course but there's no pointing letting this trouble you. However, don't let anyone steal that time from you because they presume that you're not working. You are *always* working when you're writing.

The point I want to emphasise though is to make sure that you are writing and not fiddling around with words already crafted. It's easy for a new writer to get trapped in editing mode long before it's necessary. It's also easy to become seduced by your own manuscript and to want to read it back, improve it, have a play with it. Writers like me who finish a manuscript in three months do so because we resist that urge. We write hard. We get down the main draft by drawing it out of our mental wetware and into the computer hardware.

Once you have a story down, no matter how skeletal you feel it is, you have your first draft and that's something to celebrate. That is the hardest part – finishing that original draft. If you have the luxury of time – as a new writer does, because no one has seen it yet to nag you for it – then you can set that aside for weeks to settle and come back to it with fresh eyes. I don't always have that luxury of time, so once my first draft is written only then do I read that story for the first time and my second pass means I can sharpen up the manuscript before it goes off. Now I'm fortunate to have an editorial team that then goes to work on the manuscript with me – we spend months in editing and I will read that story perhaps ten times, working through every word of it repeatedly until we have finessed it into the final shape that we all agree has the right commercial framework to please my audience. Because I have two rather brilliant editors who are highly focused on the manuscript I can be a little more gun-slingy about my approach to submission, it may sometimes arrive in a fairly raw form. But when I was a brand-new writer, I didn't have the team. I had myself and a couple of draft readers, as you will, no doubt, so it's important that you submit only the most polished work that you can. My recommendation is that you don't try to polish as you go; unless the framework is finished you can't imagine the final shape.

The best constructions, from buildings to garments and even dishes of food, begin with a solid framework – whether it's the timber before the walls go up, the pattern the clothing is cut to for accuracy of fit or the appropriately prepared ingredients that perhaps you can't see in the final dish but your senses pick up as the underlying authenticity of the food. Your first draft provides the solid storytelling framework that is going to transport readers through an exciting, emotional, absorbing journey. And then over this you will layer up the important research detail, the sensory content, colour and sparkle that makes the work memorable, commercial and thus appealing to the commissioning editor to acquire.

My belief is that if you start fleshing out before you know the final framework – or shape of your story – it could go a bit wonky and/or you can become so side-tracked and bogged down with editing and fine-tuning that you struggle to finish.

I always suggest to writers who attend my master-class – just as I will continue to remind you – to try not to look over their shoulder at yesterday's words but to push forward and to focus only on today's words. Only today's words matter.

4.

THE ESSENTIAL INGREDIENTS
OF COMMERCIAL FICTION

DEFINING COMMERCIAL FICTION

In broad terms let's define what commercial fiction is so there's no confusion about the book you have chosen to write.

At its crudest, commercial fiction boils down to money. The 'filthy dollar', loathed by literary greats, playwrights and poets, is the lynchpin that holds together the entire commercial fiction industry. It's what keeps the whole circus moving merrily along.

Everyone has to make money from commercial fiction: the creator must be paid for their fine work; the publisher must be able to make a profit from taking a risk on each new manuscript; the bookseller must be able to earn money from the books they stock, and that means that their books must fly off the shelves.

Agreed? All right, now let's make this more personal.

Your income

You must have an income from your books. You are making sacrifices, giving up your time, your energy, your love, your social life, your imagination and, possibly, your own precious dollars that are invested in the project. If you don't enter the commercial fiction world with the intention of making money I can't quite see the point. You might as well write it, print it out and give it away to friends and family – let it remain a hobby.

You have to eat, pay for your home, your car, all of your living and medical expenses, your family's needs. While writing books may not immediately cover your expenses, in time it may become your living. It now is for me. Every story I write must have a highly commercial feel to it so that I can be sure that it'll earn its place on those bookshelves in bookstores and in people's homes.

Broad appeal

Your manuscript has to appeal to the widest audience possible to maximise its potential for uptake as a 'must read' novel.

Ideally it will appeal across all demographics, all adult ages and it'll be something that both men and women enjoy. That means it's likely going to be tense, adventuresome, romantic, have a strong sense of place, larger-than-life characters and evoke strong imagery for the reader.

Make women your target audience

In today's reading environment it's wise to ensure that your novel is exceptionally appealing to women.

In fact there is a category called General Women's Fiction that the majority of commercial fiction writers want to be attached to. Why? Because women are the major purchasers of books in any household. While plenty of men buy and read books, it is women who buy and read the most books. Women also buy gifts for children, for their extended family and for friends, so appealing to them is vital.

Women tend to belong to groups, too – book groups, hobby groups, exercise groups, coffee groups, even travel groups. And in these groups they talk about everything from hair to fashion, and from health to entertainment.

Women love to share knowledge and experiences, and books are one of those conversation topics that can spark at one end of the table and consume an entire group of women as the discussion burns hot.

Nothing is quite as powerful as a woman saying to her friend, 'Read that, it's brilliant,' or 'Read this, it'll make you cry,' or even 'It's got a fantastic twist I didn't see coming.' My favourite, as I'm sure any other working novelist would agree, is this one, 'Read that, I couldn't put it down. Nothing got done until I'd finished it.'

As one of my editors pointed out, women buy all sorts of books, it doesn't matter if it's branded as women's literature, gender neutral, or tagged as serious or light. Men are, arguably, swayed by these tags – speaking generally now, most men prefer not to be reading 'a woman's book' in the same way that most men have to be persuaded to watch the romantic comedy that women enjoy so much. Let me qualify this statement.

I have plenty of male readers, and I love to hear from them, but I tap into the juggernaut of fiction for women because female readers are happy to buy, read and give books from across the whole gambit of genres. My audience has kindly followed me through fantasy, crime, children's fiction and timeslip genres and has now settled into historical romantic adventures with me. Women are generous, nimble readers and if they like something they can't help but recommend it. All the right reasons to love this category and write for it.

General women's fiction notwithstanding, the com-missioning editor at any major publishing house will be looking at your manuscript for a number of things. They'll look for its storytelling power and the quality of the writing but they'll also look with a critical eye. Does it appeal to the broadest possible demographic? Does it alienate any particular group of people? At its heart, does it make excellent entertainment? If it does, then they know it has the potential to make money for everyone involved.

WHAT DO READERS WANT FROM COMMERCIAL FICTION?

First and foremost, readers are looking for one key element: *entertainment.*

Entertaining someone doesn't mean that the reader has to be holding their bellies and laughing uproariously.

Entertainment takes many forms. Consider the range of music you enjoy. Imagine all the movies you've loved. You'll like some films because they're epic dramas that sweep you away emotionally and others because they'll take you to lands you've never seen before. Others will knock you off your feet for their amazing attention to detail of an era – it might be intriguingly historical or helplessly charming, or whimsical and delightful. There are movies that absorb you because they're full of human complexity, others grab you by the throat and won't let go because of action. Thrillers excite, and crimes and mysteries engage us for their fascinating examinations of the criminal mind. We love romance, we love comedy, and then we are more than happy to walk with characters caught up in a story of loss. We are helplessly fascinated by science fiction and fantastical worlds not of our own. Some of us, mostly teenagers – and we all went through our Stephen King phase, didn't we? – love to be frightened witless by movies. The range of movie-making is vast and the story unfolds through the actors' portrayals of the characters. The books we read are a mirror image, except that stories in books rely on the readers' imagination to animate the life and minds of the characters. And readers, providing we clue them in, are incredibly deft at doing just that.

Entertainment-seekers are more than happy to be engaged by stories in print, whether they're absorbing dramas or high-octane thrillers. The key to unlocking the reader's imagination is to picture your book as a Venus flytrap: you're luring the reader, hooking them into your story and then *snap!* you've shut them into the fictional world and are smothering them with your addictive tale. Then the captive readers will find themself so entertained that they don't want to get out.

Make sure your story is addictive with characters who are easy to fall in love with and a perfect pace for the genre. If it's a thriller it can't move slowly. If it's a big, lush romance, we don't want it to romp along too fast because we want to linger with the lovers.

Entertainment is really about absorbing your reader into the story. If they can't put the book down, that means they're entertained. They could be reading about domestic violence, *Big Little Lies*, abuse, *The Girl with a Dragon Tattoo*, serial killing, *The Silence of the Lambs*, or the aftermath of an horrific hot-air-balloon accident, *Enduring Love*. Whatever the subject matter the execution of the story must be deeply entertaining.

Allow me to labour this point once more. Please, never lose sight of the concept that your job as a novelist of commercial fiction is to captivate and entertain the reader. All of the best genre novelists know how to hook their reader into the story and never let them go.

Commercial fiction writers rarely enjoy the plaudits of literary writers. We are often left out of festival programs, particularly if we're firmly entrenched in a popular genre. We will struggle to be reviewed by the print media. As for television appearances, forget it. Unless we've killed someone with our book or saved a kitten with our book, it's just not going to happen. Radio is generous to commercial fiction writers, especially the national broadcaster and our community channels.

Biased I may be but it's a fact that we storytellers have just as much of a valuable gift as any literary writer or poet. I have tremendous admiration for poets – how do they do that? How do they pluck at my heartstrings in such a rhythmic yet succinct way and with such beautiful language? – and while I don't read much literary fiction, I would be among the first to agree that our literary novelists be protected and supported should there ever be a threat to their status as authors. In other words, I bear no grudge. I can't write poetry and I can't write a literary novel and I admire both forms enormously.

I've told you that I'm workmanlike with my writing. I don't strive for the perfect sentence using exquisite language. I adopt user-friendly sentences and a style that is *always* about feeding the story. Story is *king*, nothing takes precedence. And, dear writer, it's commercial fiction that brings home the bacon so that publishers can afford to publish a writer of beautiful prose. I'm very comfortable with and happy about that fact, so long as no one looks down their nose and sneers slightly as though commercial novelists have a particular smell about them. What you're writing is valid. We have been telling stories around campfires since the cave-dwellers first began to articulate words.

Storytelling is one of the ancient arts and it is an essential way that we pass on ideas, share our culture and entertain each other.

Commercialising stories simply means we are making it possible for everyone to enjoy them if they want to. We try not to alienate any reader by using concepts that are too hard to grasp or storytelling that is complex or a work that doesn't actually have much of a story.

We make our commercial storytelling accessible through the following:

- *Language.* Ensure easy-flowing sentences.
- *Story construction.* Make it gripping and easy to follow.
- *Subject matter.* Don't rely on the improbable tension achieved over fifty pages of staring at a cloud. Make the subject matter count.
- *Package.* The publishing company will put together an appealing cover and enticing blurb and push it out into the market with savvy sales and marketing material.

There are writers who can straddle the commercial and literary worlds: someone like Ian McEwan leaps to mind.

He writes tight, superbly wrought prose and yet his appeal is near enough mass market. I would read his shopping list for sure. I would like to read his mind. But generally commercial fiction has a 'popular' feel that literary doesn't aim to achieve.

And of course, just as importantly, while the publishers are making sure everyone in the industry can make money from your work, the reader has her own agenda for why she might buy your book. Let's assume she hasn't received that vital personal recommendation that makes word of mouth so desirable for a new book release. Let's work on the basis that your novel, with its delicious new smell and uncreased pages, has just been loaded onto bookshop shelves and has to attract the attention of shoppers on the strength of its own merit.

Everything has to be communicated via the cover image, the book's blurb and your opening chapter. What will readers be looking for?

Story Power

Commercial fiction demands that you deliver a ripping read. By that I don't mean it needs to be an enormous adventure but a story that is going to enjoy commercial success must have the power to keep drawing the reader deeper into its plot.

Tension, no matter what the genre, should keep escalating (see the 'Rhythm, Pace and Structure' chapter for a pictorial idea of what this looks like). The overarching conflict of the story, or what your main character wants, must keep getting more complex, more challenging. The very best exponents of this can make the reader hold their breath and it could be relating to a domestic scene in which there's not an iota of violence, not a raised voice or even the suggestion of a gas explosion. It could be the escalating tension that is underpinning a conversation. The reader picks up on the strain and the discord and the author keeps stretching that elasticity until it's taut and ready to snap and the reader is ready to scream. They must know what's going to happen next. That's when pages turn themselves. That's when a blockbuster is happening. That's why people remember the story, recommend the book, go back to that writer for more novels.

My editor admits to receiving 'nice' reads daily. They're sweet and feel comfy but they are not tension-filled entertainers. She can't acquire them because they will not sell in the numbers required: their sales just won't send that mighty dollar spinning around.

The Lavender Keeper is an example in my work of where I've ratcheted up the tension. My aim was to keep the reader in a permanent state of anxiety for the two lead characters. Even when Lisette was making love with Kilian – and enjoying it – there is an undercurrent of dread and fear. There's also the sense that the story is sucking you deeper into its conflict, the readers' early concerns for the characters are overwhelmed by the middle of the book, they find them in a more impossible and gripping place and they know that there's more pain to come.

My mantra is that story is king. It's what makes a reader choose to read a novel over watching a DVD or chatting with a friend on their lunch hour. It needs to move along at a steady clip and be structured strongly with highs and lows that build excitement and interest.

The word 'interest' sits tamely here but it is so important for blockbuster fiction. Your manuscript lives or dies by this sword. In this context, story power *is* interest.

Is the premise of this story interesting?

Do I feel like reading this? That's what the reader decides before they buy your book. They decide this while standing in the bookshop, lurking in the library or staring at the ebook store interface. Do these 200 words on the blurb make me want to read this novel? *Does it engage me*? And then that story must deliver on its promise that you have crafted a tale that will not only grab the reader's interest but hold it by the throat over 400-odd pages.

I firmly believe that successful commercial fiction grabs the reader's interest from the opening few paragraphs. Gone are the days of having the luxury of several chapters to set the scene and tone of your novel. Nowadays we have been trained to expect everything immediately. If news is breaking in Europe we want to read about it *right now*. If a new fashion trend is hot, we want to see it online or in store *this moment*. If there's a conversation about something highly topical, we want access to that dialogue *instantly*.

That's what the internet has done to us and it means our life expectations are following a similar course – just look at today's younger generation who want everything their parents have, but they want it right now! Don't get me started on that topic.

Back to the way commercial storytelling has developed since the new millennium. It's now imperative to fling the reader right into the guts of the conflict from the get-go. Knowing this, perhaps it's how you might consider approaching your manuscript. There's no time for exposition. It becomes a case of 'Keep up viewer, everything will make sense in time.'

I know it's a screenplay but it has some of the best story-telling dialogue ever. I'm sure you won't mind if I use the massive global success of *Breaking Bad* as an example of this approach. Especially as in film, TV and books, our aim is always to entertain our audience. Each series, and often an episode, opens with a random event. No scene setting, no detail on how we arrived at that point, or even where we are or why we're there. The viewer just goes with it – getting lost in what is arguably the finest piece of TV storytelling to date – and trusts that the characters will explain all in due course.

And of course, they do and that's why *Breaking Bad* is still so brilliant, so awarded, so talked about and so beloved. It's confident storytelling and the viewer senses that confidence and trusts it. That's what you have to do with your novel – approach your storytelling with the confidence that you will weave a captivating tale, and that when the reader glances at your opening or the blurb she will sense that confidence and if it sounds compelling, she'll trust you to deliver a great story.

Just a nod to the above – *Breaking Bad* ensures memorable characters, in a red hot story that just gets more and more dramatic, until by series six most people's hearts are ready to explode from their chests with the tension. Everything you watch feels credible and the world feels almost too real and painful at times. We know there's more pain coming for Walter and Jesse, we know our heartstrings are going to be pulled so taut we can't breathe but we are so trapped by their stories because we are helplessly invested in their lives and thus *entertained*.

Escape

Readers want to be transported from the humdrum of their lives and be thrown into a new world. They want to live vicariously through characters and live larger than their own lives. They want to be a high roller in a casino, they want to leap from planes, save lives and take risks. They want adventure and drama and to play out other people's conflicts.

Readers want to armchair travel to exotic places. They want to feel like they can taste the flavour of mint juleps in the height of summer, sense a shiver as they trudge through ice-crusted landscape, and know the glamorous feel of a hugely expensive ballgown against their skin. Readers want to be lawyers, doctors and fabulous cooks all at once. They want to hunt criminals with the police and they want to run with the criminal from the law. Readers want to hunt for treasure, ride dragons, solve a complex mystery, heroically fight the enemy, saunter through the streets of Paris or drift in a gondola through the canals of Venice. They want to switch off, just for a while, from their own life and its demands. They want to concern themselves with someone else's life for a change, a life that is more dramatic, more fabulous, more daring, more dangerous, more traumatic than their own.

For stories in blockbuster fiction must be larger than the reader's everyday life – you're allowed to have scenes of more daring, that are more breathtaking, more shocking, more wonderful in every way than real life.

Write down everything you did today. I'm guessing that unless you won the lottery or left for a big trip, or something profoundly dramatic took place, that it was a day like most others, perhaps even vaguely dull. The characters in commercial fiction can't have dull days. Their days need to be flavoured by drama, scented with conflict, spiced with sex. And then that read becomes exciting, titillating, page-turning and escapist.

Escaping into stories is why we read fiction.

Relationships

Humans are all about relationships. Ignore this at your peril if you're aspiring to write popular fiction. I'm not talking about romance here – although that is a critical ingredient that should you overlook it may lose you a vast majority of the readership. I'm referring here to ensuring there are strong, credible relationships in your story. It could be between a mother and daughter, between two brothers, between a boss and employee, between friends, even between enemies or people who find themselves on opposite sides, such as Hannibal Lecter and Clarice Starling in *The Silence of the Lambs*.

And yes, absolutely and definitely, between lovers. I'll just say Lizzie Bennett and Mr Darcy in case you need reminding. I'll chat more about Mr Darcy in just a minute.

Romance

Romance doesn't have to occur between people although it is highly desirable in genre fiction. Romance, as in Romance with a capital R, is a genre that not all of us wish to write but having a bit of romance in your stories is ideal for anyone keen to tap into commercial fiction. It's especially important if you want to roll with the juggernaut that is women's commercial fiction.

Romantic relationships are a given. But what about having a romantic setting? Readers love stories set in cities such as Paris, Florence, New York. They never tire of these settings because just about everyone loves to visit, or would one day love to visit, those cities. If you can help them get there from their armchair via the images you create for them in your writing, it can be thoroughly rewarding.

How about having a romantic era? The two world wars were such poignant times. With so much sorrow and heroism associated with them, they have become romanticised in the collective memory of readers around the world.

You could invoke romance through your subject matter, as I have. *The Tailor's Girl* revolves around the fashion of the 1920s, Savile Row in London and bespoke tailoring. This subject has a sense of romanticism about it – it's a lost art from a time of gracious couture. Meanwhile, *The Lavender Keeper's* purple fields, perfumes and settings in southern France, Paris and bomb-blitzed London prompt a universal response of romanticism.

Emotional response

They might rarely articulate this but readers want to, and need to, respond emotionally to your novel. By this I mean, is it funny? Is it sad? Do your characters display a range of emotions that the reader can connect with? Anger, bitterness, heartbreak, joy, despair – these are all valid elements to play with. You do not need to include all the emotions you can think of. But through your characters you must win an emotional response from your readers if you want your fiction to enjoy commercial success.

Readers want to observe the leading characters in their favourite novels being changed over the course of the story as a result of unfolding events. They want to share the emotional response to decisions being made and, as I tell writers who come along to my fiction classes, it is a straightforward win-or-lose situation with publishers on this point. If an editor can witness your characters transforming over the journey of the book, then the story feels as though it is in motion and that the characters are present. If your characters' inner lives remain static from beginning to end, then the story suffers and the reading experience can turn dull, no matter how exciting you think the arc of the story is.

Character is plot. This is not a throwaway comment, I say it with genuine intent. If the characters are making decisions and responding in very real ways to events, then their actions will drive the plot along. The emotional release from the characters is vital to the plot itself.

Readers genuinely want to worry for your characters. They want to laugh and cry with them, to feel bitterness and despair, to experience the disappointments and indeed the delights. They want to make love, have love made to them and to be in love through your characters.

If you haven't prompted an emotional response from your readers then you haven't done your job and you'll struggle to get a book contract. Why? Because the first reader you have to convince is an agent or editor and they know what sells.

Credibility

Even with the genres that stretch readers and ask them to suspend their disbelief, such as fantasy, magic realism and sci-fi, the author must always work hard to achieve credibility for settings, characters and events.

Writing fantasy for example requires a whole new world to be set up, one with rules that allow magic to be possible. I explore this in more detail in the 'Digging Deep' chapter.

Authors of fantasy work very hard to allow the reader to enter this new world seamlessly: to be thrown into situations with the characters where they can accept that the magical events are not only happening but that they're plausible. This plausibility is achieved through the writer deftly guiding the reader into the world, by laying out the rules and drawing them into a specially built cocoon that allows the reader to believe what they're shown.

The Lord of the Rings' Middle-earth feels legitimate because Tolkien has built it up around the reader so smoothly that we simply accept the Shire – how it looks and feels, and that hobbits populate it. We accept the hobbits without query. Credibility is about confident writing and absolute belief in your world. It is not, I might add, about having a hugely complex world – being complicated and clever doesn't make it credible. What makes it credible is that the readership can *see* it in its collective mind's eye.

Let's look at George R R Martin. I defy anyone who has read even book one of his epic series, A Song of Ice and Fire, to not be able to picture his world. For example Winterfell, which is the ancestral castle of our heroes and the seat of House Stark, effortlessly gathers clarity in our minds as the opening chapters unfold. While I freely admit that we likely all had a slightly different vision of

Winterfell in mind (until the hugely successful TV series cemented it for us), we still collectively understand the landscape that Winterfell sits within. We know it is, for the most part, cold, harsh, wooded, with mountains and ice-scapes to its north. We have a sense of harsh granite, dull grey and tough people warmed by hot springs and the godswood. George R R Martin doesn't have to say any of this. Like magic it builds around us until, if you read on through the volumes, you have a fully conceived world filled with continents. Our hearts are with the Seven Kingdoms of Westeros, of course, from that chilly North through to the soft, sun-soaked southern capital of King's Landing, or the Eyrie, that high stronghold of House Arryn, to the flat grasslands of the Dothraki. On and on it goes, building the world via the characters and their personalities and what they can grow, produce, how they live. We come to intimately understand how and why the grim, war-weathered Starks are entirely different from the Dornish people of the southernmost region of Westeros.

Of all the books that I've written, perhaps the toughest story to establish quickly with readers was Percheron. It was meant to feel exotic, a departure from the comforting and familiar medieval walled cities of the faux Europe that most of us fantasy fans are familiar with and love. For Percheron I wanted a lush, sun-drenched, salt-kissed location near the sea but with a vast and empty wilderness at its back. I used Turkey as my starting point and delved into old Constantinople for inspiration. It delivered in spades.

The wealthy and powerful eleventh century murads of the Ottoman Empire felt perfect for my world of Percheron. Just as George R R Martin and the majority of successful fantasy novelists borrow from human history, I ruthlessly borrowed from the age of the Ottomans. My sparkling capital of Pearlis on its perch overlooking the sea and the warren of city streets below feel a lot like the Topkapı Palace. To achieve this credible world, I read tonnes about the Ottomans, about life under the Murads, and about the palace and Constantinople in those early centuries. I learned about the food of the region and the time, about clothes and textiles, culture, art, social structure, lifestyle, folklore and, well, the list feels endless now that I come to ponder it. And then I went to Turkey, spent time in Istanbul and learned about life there because reading about it just wasn't enough.

I didn't let myself off the hook just because I was crafting a new world wholly from my imagination. From the opening pages of the first book, *Odalisque*, in the Percheron series, the reader begins to feel themselves walking the cobbles of those narrow alleyways and smelling the spice from the bazaar.

Having written fantasy, crime and historical, I do believe that speculative fiction is the genre where the credible immersion of the reader into a world is the most challenging. That's not to say that a crime writer or a romance writer doesn't have to work incredibly hard too. If your characters aren't credible, or your settings don't feel real enough or connect with the reader then you'll lose them very quickly.

Memorable Characters

Memorable characters are vital. Are you making it easy for your readers to connect with your cast? Can your readers respond to them? Is there empathy, hate, fear, anxiety, joy, etc for your characters?

That's your job with character – they will be the vehicle through which the story moves and why your readers keep turning the page. I'm labouring this point again because I need you to pay close attention: you want your readers to live and travel through your characters, no matter which genre you're writing in.

Long after the readers have forgotten aspects of the world of your story, it's the characters that linger in their minds.

Why does just about every female reader I know adore Mr Darcy? I'm not going to tell you why, I want you to ask yourself that question – analyse his success as a character. What is it about Mr Darcy that wins readers' hearts? Why, two hundred years on from when he was first incarnated in *Pride and Prejudice*, can this archetypal character still make women sigh? It's important you recognise what's going on with this character, so take a moment to write down your thoughts.

When you've done that, here's another one. He's not an archetype but a character who stands alone. Why do we feel ourselves helplessly onside with one of the literary world's most loathsome characters, Hannibal Lecter? If you tried to define Lecter in a few words, you'd likely come up with psychopath, serial killer and cannibal. None of these terms is endearing. And yet the man we meet in the brilliant thriller is charismatic, gently spoken, cultured, hugely intelligent, artistic, alert, romantic and, most of all, he cares about our hero, Clarice Starling. When you look at all these enviable traits, he becomes intensely likeable. Lecter wants her to crack the crime that she's investigating and while he won't deliver her all the answers, he respects her, encourages her, supports her and is angered by anyone who treats her poorly. He even protects her. And so without us being aware of it, we are able to push his heinous acts to the side as Lecter becomes someone we invest in. I found myself wanting him to escape his prison and get away with his crimes.

Here's one more memorable character: Lisbeth Salander. What an amazing antihero she is and yet from the moment this androgynous, tattooed, sociopathic misfit walks onto the pages of *The Girl With the Dragon Tattoo* I defy any reader not to be hooked on her character. She's real, she's brilliant and she's suddenly every woman who has ever been abused or felt vulnerable, plus she bites back so we love her from the moment we meet her. She's well drawn for us by Stieg Larsson and, much as we have invested in the other lead, Mikael Blomkvist, I firmly believe that every other character pales in her wake.

Essentially we love books that deliver us unforgettable characters from Fitz and the Fool featured in Robin Hobb's Farseer trilogy to Harry Potter, to Don Tillman from the enormously successful Rosie series. I could go on but risk boring you, so let's move on.

This little section is not an ad for editors but a plea for you to ask yourself some essential questions as you write your genre novel.

- *Are you showing your story, not telling your story?* We've all heard the 'show don't tell' phrase so much there's a risk it gets lost in the noise of advice. There is no better pearl of wisdom than this: your reader must be able to *see* your story unfolding in their mind's eye. They must be able to *feel* the tension and drama building. They need to be able to *hear* the voices of your characters. They should inhale and *smell* your world: whether it's coffee beans being ground in a contemporary café or the dab of lavender water in an Edwardian story. And they should be able to *taste* that sugary doughnut or that rose-flavoured Turkish Delight.
- *Are you labouring a point?* Learn to pare back. Say it once. Saying it again differently is still repeating it.
- *Are you head hopping?* Stick with one point of view per scene. Show it well through the eyes of one character. Shift to another character when you break scene. I'll cover this in more depth in a tick.
- *Are your characters interesting?* Are they entertaining?

Can they carry a reader on their shoulders and not let them get bored for 400 pages?

- *Is the dialogue important?* Does it clue the reader in an important piece of exposition or some vital fact in order to progress the action of the story?
- *Is the dialogue for your characters convincing?* Does it sound like that person talking? Does it read easily and have good rhythm?
- *Is this character vital to the story?* Are you enriching the read by painting details around the characters who are moving around in the story? In other words, can the reader *see* the world around the story itself? Is it rich in detail?
- *Is the story in motion?* Is something happening on every page of the story?
- *Is the tension of the story present and escalating?* Is there conflict?
- *Is every scene necessary?* Does it add something to the story moving forward?

Editors – and there are so many good ones available whom you can hire to help you prepare your manuscript for submission to an agent or publisher – can make sure you are addressing all these points that nourish the landscape of your story.

They will know if your manuscript is ready to be seen by a publisher. And they will guide you and ensure that you improve your novel. With an editor, you can be confident you won't burn any bridges by showing an agent or commissioning editor the story before it's ready.

For those writers who may be walking the self-publishing path, which is easier than ever now, the role of an editor cannot be underestimated. The professional editor with a proven track record in the genre in which you work can be the difference between a self-published story that drags its heels and one that breaks from the covers and goes gangbusters. The professional editor will bring their skillset to the table and make your manuscript leaner, cleaner, tidier and more robust.

WHAT *DON'T* READERS WANT?

Readers will rarely see books that feature any of the negative qualities I list below because they don't often get past the gatekeeper's desk at a publishing house or literary agency. If you want a publisher to consider your work, make sure none of the aspects noted feature in your manuscript.

An agenda

The fact that you've spent your life working with victims of domestic violence, for example, is not your readers' fault. The fact that you want to shine a spotlight on a cause that's important, especially to you, does not make it your readers' responsibility to feel obliged to read. I love animals, I want us to treat them more humanely but I don't colour my stories with that righteous message. It's my personal creed and it has no place in commercial fiction. My advice is this: do not go into writing novels because you want to advocate for a particular issue.

THE ESSENTIAL INGREDIENTS

Novels are not the vehicle for your worthy cause. You'll quickly irritate people. Save your soapbox material for a rant on social media or at your local councillor or MP. Save your writing for storytelling. No one wants to pay thirty dollars for a commercial fiction novel only to have a political message shoved down their throat or a stranger – the author – bent on pricking their social conscience. Save the lectures. Say it somewhere else. Entertain the reader.

If you feel strongly about a topic, let's say it's hedge funds, and you can show the dangers of this kind of business through your novel, just as Robert Harris did with *The Fear Index*, then it operates as a piece of entertainment and one that might also resonate on an ethical level with readers. But if you push through and preach, you'll lose your reader. *The Rosie Project* may well help people to understand aspects of Asperger's Syndrome and be more tolerant of people who display some of its markers but in the wrong hands, the subject matter probably wouldn't have worked.

I do feel the notion of successfully promoting a cause via the novel is an exception and it has to work through fabulous characterisation – as it did with Don Tillman in *The Rosie Project* and *The Rosie Effect*.

The writer's voice pushing through

This is fiction. No one wants to hear your voice. Your characters must do *all* the work.

The best way I can explain the 'push through' of the writer's voice is by enacting a role-play for the writers who attend my masterclass. I get them working on a written exercise and then I stand behind a door and stage direct the exercise that they're in the midst of doing. Firstly, it's annoying. They're trying to concentrate on what's happening in front of them on the page and yet this unembodied voice is dragging their focus.

This is what pushing through the storytelling means. If you're busy focusing your reader on the world of the story you're building and populating that story with characters they are intrigued with, then what you absolutely don't want is some stranger – that's you – popping into the story and saying 'Oh, by the way, concentrate on this bit, it's really good'. Then you drag them away from the storytelling and focus their attention on you, your opinions, your knowledge, your voice.

Unless it is coming out of a character's mouth or it is something a character can express in thought or action, it must be deleted. It's only what your characters can see, think, do or say that is relevant.

Poor writing

This is an obvious point really but still, it needs to be said. Poor writing encompasses everything from a clumsy style, to red herrings and loose ends, to poorly developed characters, to storylines that go nowhere and stories with unsatisfying endings.

Poor writing doesn't usually get past the editorial desk of the major publishers unless the story itself – which is king, remember – is superior in some way. By that I mean that it must be original, titillating, have enormous mass-market appeal and so on. I will not name names by way of example of poor writing because I'm not a person who takes a baseball bat to other writers. Anyone who does that has clearly not sat in front of a keyboard with 500 blank pages to fill with addictive storytelling.

However, I'm sure many of you have novels that come to mind that fit the poor-writing category. The writing is not skilled but the story does the heavy lifting. For a novelist to have ongoing success and a long career they must aim to improve skills across the board, just as most of us do with each new book we craft.

All that said and done, don't be contemptuous of the straightforward read either. You are writing popular fiction – you're writing for everyone, so don't get carried away with flowery sentences or complex styling of your writing.

Time and again I see first-time writers reaching too hard to sound writerly. Their sentences are blousy and overwritten, they're full of unnecessary words or labour a point. I used to make the mistake – and my editor will probably smile and say I still do – of repeating myself. I would write something and then say it differently because I felt the need to reinforce my point. But it is *not* necessary. The reader caught it the first time.

Readers are fabulously intelligent creatures. When they read, they are paying attention to what you've written.

You can tell you're reading something that's been over-written when, as a reader, you feel a bit of a cringe coming on. The writer is straining to paint a picture for you, which is admirable, but laying it on so thick you're choking with florid images. This is not terminal, it is easily fixed if you take the time to study the bestselling writers in your genre who are published by the top imprints. Read a few of their novels and you'll begin to see that they write evocatively but concisely with no odd phrasings or language choices to stumble over.

Flowery prose has no place in commercial fiction. Write succinctly, in as few words as you can, in a simple style that everyone can understand and using straightforward language that does not send the reader scurrying for a dictionary. A journalist at a daily newspaper writes in a style that people across all demographics can understand. That's how you should aim to write.

No conflict

There are no rules in commercial fiction, except perhaps this one: you cannot have a story without conflict.

In the same way that humankind cannot survive without oxygen or water, and I cannot survive without new winter boots each season, or chocolate each day, a story cannot be in motion without conflict deep at its core.

You may like to consider conflict as being the engine

room of the story. It is what drives your story forward.

Imagine two neighbouring houses belonging to two couples, the Smiths and the Joneses, and you can choose to be a fly on the wall at only one of them.

The Smith household when you swoop in is calm. The childless couple is sitting on the sofa with a mug of tea each and quietly talking, smiling gently, their dog at their feet. Their voices are low, just loud enough for each other, and they're sharing how their day has gone. They're even holding hands. With your amazing super powers you glean that both have experienced an uneventful, pleasant enough time at work.

You fly to the house of the Joneses. They're in the kitchen and an argument is in full roar. Voices are raised, body language is far from comfortable, threats are being made. Mrs Jones picks up a nearby cup and flings it at Mr Jones, who ducks just in time. He's clearly enraged and you watch him straighten and stride towards his wife.

Which of the houses would you rather observe?

Yes, of course, you want to remain with the Joneses. Why? Because it's far more interesting to observe a situation of conflict than it is to yawn and watch a scene where nothing much is happening and nothing much is going to happen.

And flies on the wall aside, humans are hard-wired to be curious. We cannot help ourselves. We want to know what is going on. It's why we helplessly slow down in traffic at the scene of an accident and why we sit, horrified but transfixed, when scenes of global disasters are being transmitted live through our televisions.

Happy, relaxed, content people like the Smiths do *not* make good viewing and they certainly do not make addictive, pacy reading.

Too often I've heard editors bemoaning a dearth of conflict in the manuscripts that they read on submission. They not only search for signs of conflict but with an increasing concern for whether there will be any conflict powerful enough to drag the mass-market audience with it.

I don't write the perfect story. I certainly improve with each novel and I can recall as recently as *Fields of Gold* when my editor and I realised we'd hit a flat spot in the manuscript. She saw it first and drew my attention to it. The story was effectively treading water. That's when a story is drowning and you have to learn how to recognise it.

'What's the worst thing that could happen here between these two people?' my editor asked me.

It was a powerful question. I'm sure I looked like a cartoon character for a moment as I my face crumpled in on itself in a deep frown. What she wanted from me was something dramatic. I moved to the most daunting situation that this particular woman in this particular scenario could face and, almost in disbelief, I cast the idea at my editor and wondered with held breath how she'd respond.

'Yes! That's it!' she came back at me. 'That's perfect. It would be terrifying for a woman in her position. That's what we should do.'

And that's what we did. People are looking for drama. It's no good holding back in commercial fiction. You have to be bold and go for it. The most dramatic event is what you're chasing. Commercial fiction is not about the most realistic situation – it's about the most incredible or heart-stopping or unbelievable or most romantic, the most daring, most frightening, most breathtaking scenario. It's these dramatic events that make blockbuster fiction tick.

If you don't have conflict in your tale, you don't have a story to tell.

I'll cover this in more detail in Chapter 6: Character, but here are some questions that all commercial fiction writers – planners, freefallers and everyone in between – should seriously consider following as they set out on their new manuscript.

- What motivates your prime character/s? Why?
- Who or what is the obstacle? Why?
  Not even a raging freefaller like myself would set out on the journey of a novel of 100 000 words or so without knowing these two elements, because together they form the main conflict for my piece of fiction.

5.

HOOKING YOUR READERS

———————

For mass-market fiction – and this is where the dollars are – publishers are looking for books that plunge the reader straight to the heart of the action. Movies and increasingly good TV shows are great exponents of this concept that as commercial novelists we can learn from.

Look at the James Bond movies. Their openings are always heart-stopping, full of tension and you don't care that you don't immediately understand what's happening, you know you'll catch up fast. It's not only the high-octane thrillers that begin this way, even quieter genres can tip you straight into conflict. An example might be Bridget Jones arriving at her parents' house for the dreaded Christmas turkey buffet – you can feel the tension building. And blockbuster TV shows are no different – *Breaking Bad*, *Game of Thrones*, *House of Cards*, *True Detective*, *24* – they all fling you into conflict and don't waste time with exposition and scene-setting.

WRITING YOUR OPENING PARAGRAPH

One method I use in my opening paragraph is to slam the reader straight into a crisis point for a lead character. Then there's no confusion for the reader: they know where the story begins. The crisis point ensures immediate tension and hooks the reader.

Exercise

1. Grab a magazine. I find something like *National Geographic* works really well for this exercise.

2. Open the magazine and randomly select a picture. It may be a person, it could be a landscape, it's more than likely a scene with movement in it. It doesn't matter what it is. Don't try to control what you pick – be spontaneous.

3. Set your alarm for fifteen minutes' time. Be strict with time not because you have to write fast to produce a good opening but because I'm suggesting you go with gut instinct and just write whatever comes to your mind first.

4. Set yourself a word count, maybe 400 words. It only needs to be a few paragraphs for this exercise.

5. Start writing. Jump straight into something dramatic, even if the image isn't full of drama. Make the moment feel like a watershed moment or a crisis point; a creative writer can make a puddle of water become a tense moment. It doesn't matter if what you write doesn't relate to the image. The picture is there to help trigger your opening.

Try this exercise a few times using different pictures. Go on, surprise yourself at how good you get at it.

If you practise writing random opening paragraphs regularly, you'll quickly start to see an improvement in their quality and emotional punch. And, as you progress, see if you can answer these question:

- Have I introduced a lead character?
- Have I thrown the reader into a moment of crisis that involves this lead character?
- Do I give any idea of who they are? What they do for a living, for example? Age?
- Have I clued in the reader as to where we are?
- Can the reader glean the era? Is this a contemporary setting? Is it historical and if so, roughly when? Are we in a make-believe world?

And just maybe after all the practice, you'll be able to thread into these 400 words some idea of time frame, for example season, time of day, what drama might be unfolding next, who else is important to this story.

Practise, practise, practise.

The way you write now is different to how you'll be writing in one year, five years, ten years. I look back at my first novel – the one that's still selling all over the world and in various languages – and I could cringe. My writing style back then feels like the blows of a sledgehammer. But that was as good as I could be in the year 2000. Within a couple of years my stories were getting better, my characters were more complex. Now I'm writing books that have a strong sense of place, my characters can entertain a big audience with their decisions and ensuing adventures, my novels are more ambitious, written with a more confident tone. I've been learning on the job and that's how it should be. I'm always improving and you will too, if you practise.

Go now and find your favourite five books of, let's say, the past two or three years. Read their blurbs and then, importantly, their opening paragraphs. Email me if they don't crackle and fizz. I'll bet they do!

One of my favourite books of all time is *Tigana*, a fantasy novel by French-Canadian author Guy Gavriel Kay. A few years back *The Australian* asked me to write about the novel that changed me.

Tigana is a book that I bought and devoured because of its opening. From that first sentence – a long one, too – I sensed I was embarking on a special journey.

The epic nature of the storyline, the setting reminiscent of Italy in the Middle Ages, the fabulously drawn and powerful characterisations aside, this book didn't just stay with me, it changed me. *Tigana* pushed me on to a new career path.

In the first fifty or so words I learned who, what, when, where and why. Kay conveyed all that information effortlessly. How did he show me so much in so few words?

I was in my mid thirties and just beginning to have the awakening of my own desire to write a novel. When you read the work of a master craftsman, it provokes pause because it's intimidating, often disheartening.

Tigana, first published in 1990, is a magnificently realised fantasy tale that reads like historical fiction and could be considered literary in its construction. It has a haunting storyline and sparkling characters – each with their own complex motivations.

It elicited heartfelt emotion from me. I wept towards the end and now, as a seasoned writer, I understand how hard that level of emotional response is to achieve. *Tigana* lured me back into the world of fantasy that I had left behind as a child.

I was – and still am – daunted by *Tigana* but I was also fantastically inspired.

Kay wrote this before the digital era had taken hold. So I think it's valid to mention that it was written at a time when flinging the story into conflict wasn't as necessary as it is today and he uses a more sweeping style of writing.

Even so, in just fifty words we derive the following.

We know the season. We get a feel for the landscape and recognise it, so we know we're in a world that is not so markedly different from our own. We learn an important man has died – a ruler of a city. We know that this man died angry in exile and, as a reader, we wonder how that anger, which has been mentioned for good reason, will impact the story. *We are clued in to the conflict.* We know that the dead man was the Duke of Astibar, so now we have a place in our world and know that this sort of European rank exists. We get smells and visuals, tastes and colours, all in this one sentence.

I count six important clues being laid out in one sentence, in which Kay has set up much of what we need to know about the world we will be moving through, and he has already given us a character. We don't know how much we will learn about this duke but the fact that Kay opens his prologue with a prince on the verge of a battle to the death and begins chapter one with Sandre gives you a feeling that they will be linked and are important.

This is what Guy Gavriel Kay has to say about his opening sentence: 'I wanted to start a book about subterfuge and deception with an outright lie – and the first sentence of chapter one does that.'

Intrigued? You should be. It's a fabulous story.

WRITING YOUR BLURB

Our books are competing with a vast array of other entertainment, especially the internet. Consumers are spoilt for choice when it comes to deciding how to spend their money on entertainment. There's music, theatre, sport, concerts, cinema, TV; the list goes on.

No matter the genre, a novel needs to be robust and addictive to compete effectively in the marketplace – and buyers must see the purchase of a novel as a valid piece of entertainment. Today's entertainment is faster paced and instantly gratifying. We do not want our next generation to turn away from books, we want our children to love their picture books, then their middle readers and then their YA novels. As writers it is our responsibility to keep people entertained and returning to reading, no matter how much reality TV demands our audience's attention.

Even more important, perhaps, is how a potential reader buys a book. The cover is vital. Authors have little and sometimes no control over a cover. Yes, the publisher will consult with you but, particularly when you're starting out, they're being polite. A publisher's sales and marketing team will decide what goes on the front cover of your book. So you must concern yourself with what you can control – and it's not the cover, unless of course you're self-publishing in which case you are in charge of it all.

It's useful to focus on the blurb. This is your domain whether you've already got a publishing deal or you're still trying to get one. You must wrestle this skill of writing a blurb into surrender because as a new writer it is most likely going to be the first thing that prospective publishers read when you're pitching that manuscript.

Learning the skills of writing blurbs is one of the

toughest to acquire. If it's any consolation I work harder at this part of my job than any other, I reckon.

We practise this skill in my masterclass because I know from hard experience that writers should be able to capture the essence of their story in 200–250 words. When we set out no one believes they can do it, the breadth of their story feels huge, and yet by the end of the week's masterclass everyone can distil their story into a snappy and appealing blurb. Get focused.

This is what you have to remember though when writing a back cover blurb or even a short blurb to pitch to publishers: you are not *re-telling* the story in short form, it is not a synopsis; rather, you are *selling* the story to a potential reader.

Your task here is to tantalise, not summarise.

Think hard about what it is in your story that might make someone want to read it. Knowing your theme is helpful. Themes can often be summarised in one or two words – betrayal, for instance. If you can bed down your key theme, then you have a cornerstone on which to build your blurb. Here's a helpful checklist:

- Don't mention more than three characters.
- Share the conflict.
- Allude to setting and era.
- Hint at the drama that's going to unfold.
- Be clear about the book's genre.

SOME BLURB EXAMPLES

Here's what runs on the back cover blurb for *The Lavender Keeper*:

> Lavender farmer Luc Bonet is raised by a wealthy Jewish family in the foothills of the French Alps. When the Second World War breaks out he joins the French Resistance, leaving behind his family's fortune, their home overrun by soldiers, their lavender fields in disarray.
>
> Lisette Forrestier is on a mission of her own: to work her way into the heart of a senior German officer – and to bring down the Reich in any way she can. What Luc and Lisette hadn't counted on was meeting each other.
>
> When they come together at the height of the Paris occupation, German traitors are plotting to change the course of history. But who, if anyone, can be trusted? As Luc and Lisette's emotions threaten to betray them, their love may prove the greatest risk of all.

This blurb is 133 words. And while I know it can be improved because I'm five years on skillswise, it does provide the following information:

- Characters: we are introduced to the two key characters. We know who they are by name and at what point they are in their lives.

- Conflict: we know what their individual conflicts are at the time of meeting them.
- Setting: we know where in the world we are.
- Era: we know in which historical period the story is set.
- Drama: we know the overarching conflict affecting them, i.e. the occupation of Paris and German plotters trying to change the course the world is on.
- Genre: we know it's going to be sweeping drama with romance and adventure.

That's a lot of helpful information in just over 100 words. And it has assisted readers to make a quick and enthusiastic decision that this is sounding like the sort of gripping story they want to get lost in.

Gripping is a key word! That's what you're aiming for with your blurb. How to crystallise your 500 pages and up to 130 000 words into a pithy and gripping 200-word blurb.

Could you ignore this blurb?

> One windy spring day in the Chilterns Joe Rose's calm, organised life is shattered by a ballooning accident. The afternoon, Rose reflects, could have ended in mere tragedy, but for his brief meeting with Jed Parry. Unknown to Rose, something passes between them – something that gives birth in Parry to an obsession so powerful that it will test to the limits Rose's beloved scientific rationalism,

threaten the love of his wife Clarissa and drive him
to the brink of murder and madness.

Eighty-two words.

Enduring Love by Ian McEwan is one of my favourite
reads.

How about this powerful blurb for *Birdsong* from
Sebastian Faulks?

> A novel of overwhelming emotional power, *Birdsong*
> is a story of love, death, sex and survival. Stephen
> Wraysford, a young Englishman, arrives in Amiens
> in northern France in 1910 to stay with the Azaire
> family, and falls in love with unhappily married
> Isabelle. But, with the world on the brink of war,
> the relationship falters, and Stephen volunteers to
> fight on the Western Front. His love for Isabelle
> forever engraved on his heart, he experiences the
> unprecedented horrors of that conflict – from
> which neither he nor any reader of this book can
> emerge unchanged.

Note it's just shy of 100 words.

Or this? *The Kite Runner* by Khaled Hosseini:

> Afghanistan, 1975: Twelve-year-old Amir is desper-
> ate to win the local kite-fighting tournament and
> his loyal friend Hassan promises to help him. But

neither of the boys can foresee what will happen to Hassan that afternoon, an event that is to shatter their lives. After the Russians invade and the family is forced to flee to America, Amir realises that one day he must return to Afghanistan under Taliban rule to find the one thing that his new world cannot grant him: redemption.

Eighty-two words that make you to want to read the book, right?

You will not work harder than on the 200 words you write for your blurb.

Nailing this crucial piece of marketing requires a deep focus on what the main thrust of the story is. It forces you to be ruthless in your choice of words and to be succinct. The skill of blurb-writing cannot be underestimated and you should be prepared to gnash your teeth over it.

THE IMPORTANCE OF CAPTURING YOUR READER'S ATTENTION

The blurb and your opening paragraphs are of paramount importance, they provide the reason for the reader's purchase. You will never get an editor, a book buyer or a library borrower to give your book their time if you can't excite them with the blurb and your opening paragraphs.

A potential buyer walks into a bookstore and initially is attracted to a cover: if they don't like the cover, it's hard to get someone to consider it. We should not fool ourselves with the adage 'Never judge a book by its cover' because, invariably, people do judge books by their covers. That said, cover design is out of your control. Accept that the publishing team has the experience and the expertise. It possesses the marketing nous and years at the sales coalface to know what the bookseller needs on their shelf and what the consumer wants at this moment. You worry about the words and trust the team to take care of the cover. They won't always get it right, they're human after all. But they'll get it right more times than not and if you go on to publish regularly and successfully together, the publisher will nail down what design direction works for your books.

If you're self-publishing, then you need to canvass your choice of cover to as many people as you can. Not just friends and family but librarians, booksellers and readers – strangers! You need to be confident in your ability to gauge opinion from potential readers and that will be possible if you speak with people who are not personally invested in your success.

Anyway, back to the bookstore. Let's presume the cover's terrific and a potential buyer has picked up your book and is now considering it. Invariably they'll flip the book to the back cover and read that blurb. If the blurb sounds intriguing, then, with few exceptions, people are going to open that cover.

And here you are now, teetering on the precipice of a book sale. It all comes down to that magnificently written opening.

The customer will read the first few paragraphs, perhaps the opening page, and very possibly they'll go on to the second page. But it's those opening sentences that make up the mind of the buyer. This all happens in a few heartbeats, of course, and your book is then placed back on the shelf or it walks away in the hands of the buyer. But it's your opening that will seal the deal. Even if the blurb is entertaining, the discerning buyer who is about to part with precious dollars will invariably rely on their own judgement, and that comes down to your beginning.

So, you must work hard on it.

Let's not ignore ebooks. More and more people are buying ebooks. Your opening is even more vital in the digital space because there's none of that wonderful tactile contact with the book that a print buyer has. Customers are relying on an image of the cover – one that they can't touch and feel for its silkiness, its embossing or shiny lettering. They are also relying on the book excerpt that the e-bookstore provides. Almost the entire purchase decision rests on the entertainment potential of your opening chapter. If you meander, if you drift, if your writing is ordinary, or if you fail to introduce a lead character in whom we can invest or who can clue us in to the conflict, then you won't immerse them swiftly in your fictional world. Then you've lost that buyer and they've already scrolled to the next option.

That first chapter is essentially an extended blurb that must sell the e-reader on the rest of the story that lives behind the opening chapter. As my editor succinctly puts it, 'It has to work its arse off' – and she's right.

Remember also that the commissioning editor at a publishing house is the most important reader of all. Without winning this person's interest, if you don't make them want to read on, then you'll never get to that bookstore shelf. Every commissioning editor will *always* read your first chapter so there really is nowhere to hide; your opening must sparkle.

6.

CHARACTER

You've probably heard mentioned that 'character is plot', yes? I subscribe strongly to this idea. Here's what it means to me:

- Your characters create the plot.
- Whatever decision your characters are making, whatever they are saying and doing is what will keep the story moving along.
- If the characters are not boring, then your story will not be either.
- Characters – not you – carry the burden of the story. They have to leap off the page in a robust, striking way that ensures reader attention is caught, trapped and then invested in your lead character(s) especially. But it's their lives that make the story. You, the author, must remain in the background.

Get your characters right and the battle for attention is effectively won – your readers will let go of the humdrum of daily life and escape with the novel. So you must ensure your characters earn their place in your story.

You know if you haven't got your characters right if:
- They defy the traits you've set up.
- They disappoint the reader through their actions.
- They are not named well.

Miss the mark with your characters and the setting, world, story arc, punchy dialogue and beautiful writing – no matter how absorbing – will never be enough for readers.

Please work very hard on your characters. Here are some pointers I've learned.

- *Characters need to develop through your book.* At all costs avoid having them in a state of stasis, not being changed by the events that occur. Show how their experiences during the story affect their approach to life and the decisions they make. Character development is one of the most important aspects that the commissioning editor will be looking for when she considers your submission. This is a win-or-lose situation. No character development? No contract!

- *Your reader must be able to engage with your characters.* Some of your characters are going to be difficult to like, and that's good. We need some characters who are prickly, who disappoint now and then, or who are genuine villains. These are

the characters you're going to enjoy writing and
developing because they usually provide the most
interest in terms of craft and reading experience.
The heroic characters are, somehow, easier to build.
There is the danger that these goodies, if I can call
them that, can be dull if you don't work hard to
rough them up a bit, give them some edginess,
some faults that your reader recognises, perhaps
even some darkness.

- Being engaged by a character doesn't mean
the reader has to like them but they have to be
interested in them. They must be fascinated by their
actions and decisions. That's when they invest in
the story.

- I cite Lisbeth Salander once again. She's far from
perfect, in fact she's dark at times, but a true hero
for the book and someone who keeps developing,
keeps surprising the reader.

- As I've noted earlier, in commercial fiction *your
characters can be larger than life*. In fact I'd suggest
you go ahead and make them just a bit better
looking, or a little less attractive, or funnier, or
more daring, or more pithy or more feeble than
the average person. These people are going to have
to leap out from the pages and grab the interest of
a reader sitting on a train or lounging at home or
soaking in a tub or slothing by a pool. They need
to demand attention and then pin down the reader

by being addictive. Your reader must want to turn the page to find out what the characters are going to do next.

LEAD CHARACTER

Your lead characters, particularly your hero/heroine, are going to carry the weight of the story on their shoulders, so equip the characters solidly. Give them depth, give them pain, give them great highs. Punish and reward. Build them, layering the character with more information as the reader moves through the tale. Let the reader experience their growth.

Give them strong reasons for their decisions and know some, if not all, of their backstory, even if you don't use it – have some idea of their motivations. For example, an orphaned child may view life through a different lens than one who has grown up with two doting parents. Similarly, someone who has had to face tremendous adversity – illness, injury, emotional upheaval – will likely behave differently to a given situation than someone who has led a protected, more cosseted lifestyle.

Some writers aren't sure who their lead character is. A useful yardstick is to identify the person who has the most at stake – indeed, this is likely to be the person who will suffer the most in your story. Seek them out. They will surely be at the centre of the conflict, so you need to know *what they want and why*. That's the motivation I spoke about earlier. What is driving this person?

For instance, while there are three lead characters in *The Lavender Keeper*, the person's life we're most invested in is Luc's. I write just as many words about Lisette and only slightly fewer about Markus Kilian, who is vital to the story, but without Luc there is no *The Lavender Keeper*. Luc is important enough to be the bearer of the book's title. I even wrote a second volume that continues his adventure, exploring his need to find out what happened to his childhood family. He is the one with the most at stake.

Even though *Nightingale* is about lovers, family, war and lost friendships, it is ultimately about the life of Claire Nightingale and so we experience the war and its aftermath through her. I had to write my opening chapter a few times before I realised Claire was the true narrator even though I set out to write the story of Jamie Wren.

The Last Dance uses a third-person perspective but is told entirely from the view of Stella Myles. It was only after I'd finished it that I wondered whether I should have written it in first person. In the past I've preferred following various lives and perspectives but, thirty books into my career, I realise that I am narrowing down the viewpoint to the person who suffers the most in my stories. I am now writing a novel entirely in first person, which is a new challenge for me. Regardless of the story perspective, I do know who my major character is because I know who has the most at stake, who suffers the most and who carries the story on their shoulders.

This includes knowing my lead's nemesis. Who is standing in the way of your lead? So arrives another key character. It is every bit as important to develop your antagonist, to give them a rich background.

In a bigger cast, you may have several leads, each with a different nemesis. Look at *Big Little Lies,* the immensely enjoyable novel by Liane Moriarty. We're following the stories of three different women with their unique problems.

If you're writing a story with a big cast – fantasy, for example, tends to favour larger character groups – then please devote equal amounts of care to all of your characters, just as you might if you were writing a story with two leads.

Again I shall say that every character must earn their place in your story. If they're in it, then you must make sure that your readers understand why and then allow the reader to get to know them.

SECONDARY CHARACTERS

There will be a host of secondary characters and they too need their stories to fill out as the tale moves along. Readers want to understand what makes characters tick and why they do what they do. Secondary characters often bob up unexpectedly, and that's fine and normal. Don't be fearful of this. Let them stay and play, in fact let them rip – see where they take you. In every novel I've written

I think it would be fair to say that I've had a secondary character appear out of nowhere. On most occasions I've considered this character a plot device – someone to get me from A to B, whatever those plot points are.

In each instance that secondary character proved to be worthier than their 'plot device' tag, they were more than a cameo. The best example I have of this occurring in my own writing is Fynch from the series The Quickening. Fynch is the gong boy for the palace with the unsavoury task of climbing the drop latrine to clean the walls from ground to the top where the royal apartments are. He's tiny enough to clamber up the narrow opening and the waste burns his skin but he has to do this filthy work to help keep his family going. He's invisible to the palace staff and inhabitants because of his dirty work; people hardly notice him. However, Fynch is observant beyond the natural curiosity of others, with a memory that never loses anything. And he knows a lot more about the palace than most might credit the gong boy. While cleaning the latrine tunnel leading into the royal apartments one day, he overhears something terrifying. And that was his original reason for coming into being. That's all I needed Fynch to do: overhear this news and be able to pass it on to my heroic lead character. I thought he'd disappear after that but how wrong I was. Fynch stuck around. He began to claim more scenes until I was including him in chapters as a matter of course, until he became one of the most important characters, until he roamed through three big books and, ultimately, became the unexpected hero in the finale.

I began to receive mail about Fynch after people had read volume one of The Quickening. It went something along the lines of 'If you dare touch a hair on his head, you will be made accountable'. It was such an eye-opener. Someone I'd originally deemed an entirely unimportant character – someone with a walk-on walk-off part – began to develop and become addictive to the reader.

The secondary, unimportant character takes over and is no longer a device but someone the audience fully invests in.

Allowing characters to arrive and flex their muscles is worth it. They will show you soon enough if they're important to the novel.

Here are a range of brief exercises you can do now or return to later. You can also repeat them any time – they're always helpful, even for the most experienced novelist.

Exercise

Turn to your magazines again. Pick out the first face you don't recognise in one of the pages. Don't overthink this, don't try to choose one, just settle on the first unfamiliar face you see. Build a character profile for the person you're looking at.

- Who are they?
- What do they do for a living?
- How do they spend their days?

- What are they aspiring to? (This may be particularly relevant if they're young.)
- What are this person's dreams? If they're old, what did they dream of achieving? What stopped them achieving those dreams if they didn't reach their goals?
- Regardless of the success of their prospective or dashed dreams, what drives them now?
- Whom do they love?
- What matters most to them?
- Describe them.
- Where do they live?
- Where were they born?
- What was their childhood and upbringing like?

Planners might build a profile for their characters as a matter of course. I don't write it down but at the back of my mind I subconsciously build this sort of profile for each character as I go about the business of writing the story. Whichever sort of writer you are, these are very helpful questions to answer about your characters because they will help you understand how they'll behave in a situation, in particular why they may behave in a certain manner when under stress.

Exercise

Write an opening paragraph – I suggest you keep it to 100 words and use a lead character. Base the opening paragraph on this line:

He/she looked up, alarmed.

This prompt will help to trigger you into action so you don't spend the next ten minutes thinking about what to write.

In this single paragraph you should be able to write about who the character is, what the conflict is, where they are and who and what is around them.

Okay, grab a pen and paper or turn on your computer. You've got ten minutes from now. Go!

Exercise

Write down two or three aspects of yourself that few people know about. Nothing mundane, please. Do you have an interesting hobby or any curious quirks to your personality? What about any syndromes, fetishes and obsessions?

There's no need to share this with anyone, of course. Do this in the privacy of your own writing space and trash it later if you want, just be sure to be honest and dig deep, go back into childhood even.

You may be surprised by what comes out.

Exercise

Takes the previous exercise to the next level by doing it with a stranger. It's best you don't know them too well – someone from a writing or reading group would be perfect as they will be sympathetic to your goal (and hopefully willing to open up). You might like to return the favour. Take ten minutes to interview each other. You don't want to know that they love their family, that they live in such-and-such city. None of that is interesting. What is interesting is that this person has no sense of smell – how has that shaped their life? Or that this person is a volunteer firefighter – what goes through their head when the fires are raging? Or that this person grew up in a household with a violent father, or that they have synaesthesia, or that they can't step on the cracks in the pavement. That's what you're after – interesting and character-defining stuff away from the norm.

EVERYONE HAS A STORY TO TELL AND INSPIRATION IS EVERYWHERE

What should be becoming apparent for you, I hope, is the understanding that everyone is interesting, even the most outwardly 'ordinary' people.

Scratch the surface and, lurking below, often quite deep in our psyche, are aspects of ourselves that make us far more intriguing than we seem at first glance. Eidetic memories, syndromes with curly names, quirks without names, phobias and skills – hunt these down.

Suddenly your neighbour, the supermarket checkout lady, the guy at the petrol station will come alive. If you get behind the public façade of a person, you will hear extraordinary stories just as I have about obsessions, tragedies, daydreams and wild events.

I've included the final exercise of this chapter to give you an understanding of how a character can be developed. Chatting to everyday people about their extraordinary experiences and traits will reinforce the fact that everyone is interesting. And just like in real life, this is what you have to achieve with your novel's characters. Let your friend from reading group, the girl at the checkout, the waiter, the postman and the librarian inspire you.

You may have learned that the person you spoke to has travelled widely or was born in an exotic destination during the Second World War. Plumb these experiences. You may discover that they're one of identical triplets or that they have expertise in nanotechnology. There are myriad possibilities. Find out what makes them a bit different and, apart from appreciating how interesting even the most ordinary person is, you may even acquire some ideas for personality traits for future characters.

I'm not saying every person in your pages must be fantastically interesting because that would be distracting. No, I'm simply asking you to form an appreciation that everyone has a backstory and even though they are an ordinary person in the eyes of the community, it doesn't stop them from being interesting in a number of ways. If you are going to have a waitress as a key character, don't feel bound by her simple background and everyday life. You'll be delighted by how fascinating a character can become because of the way you handle their characteristics. A simple tic, clumsiness or a tendency to get flustered – these qualities can be captivating for the reader.

These details will make a character infinitely more interesting to a reader than, say, good looks. Mr Darcy, for instance, is desirable for his looks and his wealth but it's his failings that make him more intriguing. Later, it's his passion for Elizabeth Bennett hidden by aloofness and arrogance that makes us love him.

It helps that Colin Firth immortalised Darcy in the BBC production of *Pride and Prejudice*. For many, his portrayal eclipses the original work, so many watched the series but hadn't read Austen's novel. However, who cares? It has sent lots of people scurrying to read the book. Frankly I wore out my videotape in the 1990s – it may have been that scene of him climbing out of the lake in his white fencing shirt (blushing now at the memory) that did it. I had to buy the series on DVD so I could watch over and over without wearing anything out other than my husband and twin sons' patience. If I had to choose one movie or television clip to take with me to a desert island, it would be this one. If you're reading this, Colin, I know it's annoying but we love you in a wet white shirt while you stammer and repeat polite questions – and yes, I will run away with you.

Anyway, back to writing and imbuing your character with traits. Don't crowd in too many. The mere fact that someone has a pronounced limp might be enough. How did the limp come about and how has it shaped that person's life? Was it through illness? Has it been present since childhood? Has the person been bullied because of it? It has presumably prevented them from experiencing many things. If so, what and how has not being able to be viewed as 'normal' affected this person? All of these questions might come together to form a character who is sensitive, aggressive, bitter, courageous and fragile. You get to choose how they have coped and how it has shaped them but remember, they get to show the reader.

Dashing and delicious, or evil and ugly is one thing but what makes the character stay with you is when you get below their skin and learn that the dashing and delicious guy is someone who likes to taste blood or that the evil and ugly fellow likes to save baby birds that fall out of nests each spring. How about the serial killer who cries at animal cruelty, the teacher who hates children? Keep this firmly in mind when crafting your characters.

All of that said, it's what the characters do in your story that keeps the tale moving along and the reader turning pages.

Readers love to loathe the villain as much as they love to invest in the heroes of tales. Characters are what reach out and touch the reader more strongly than any other aspect of your story. I know that sounds obvious but it needs to be reinforced so that a new writer to all forms of fiction pays attention to character development.

Without character there is no emotion, no story whether they're human, animal – or alien.

DESCRIBING YOUR CHARACTERS

You know how it is when you go to see 'the movie of the book'? It can be disappointing when your own image of the lead character is wildly different to the director's. The point is, everyone in the audience will have their own idea of what the character looks like.

Your job as an author is to give the reader an outline of your character without being so constraining that their imagination is not allowed to do most of the work. Remember, once you let go of your book, you let go. The characters become real in the reader's mind and their vision of each character is the *only* one that matters. Yours is the starting point but, ultimately, it's irrelevant. So definitely give some framework of how your characters look but leave room for the reader to participate. Trust their imagination.

It's helpful to consider three physical traits of your characters that you may mention in your novel. This could be height, colour of eyes, how they wear their hair, the shape of their face, the type of nose they have, whether their ears stick out, what their voice sounds like, the fact they have large hands or ankles that look like they were sculpted for an angel.

The trick is not to load too many in. Leave room for the reader. Some skilled writers don't bother to provide any description at all; they are confident that through the course of the story the reader will develop a strong sense of the character, picking up ideas here and there are the tale unfolds. That really is the best way. But while you develop your skills it's perfectly feasible and desirable that you include visual aspects to give the reader a sense of the character she is about to share her life with.

The other 'don't' is don't tell us she has long, chestnut

hair. *Show us*. How are you going to do that? Think about the ways you might:

- Describe her brushing her hair.
- Describe her running her fingers through it.
- Describe someone else noticing her hair.
- Describe how it moves in the breeze.
- Describe how her child likes to play with it or how her lover likes to feel it on his skin.

Describe the hair left on the bathroom floor after she's blow dried. For heaven's sake, just don't write 'Her chestnut hair falls past her shoulders'.

Characters may arrive in your mind fully shaped or frustratingly misty. So long as they feel present and relevant to you, then you must not ignore them. They are asking for their place in your story. My personal experience is that I've never deliberately shaped a character for a story and, by the same token, I've never pre-prepared a character to then go looking for a scene or a story to shape around him. If you agree that character is plot, then your characters and the story that emerges from their lives and actions go hand in hand and seem, rather cleverly, to shape each other – if you'll let them.

Let me underscore that going with the flow with your characters is something that we all learn. Not being too rigid or controlling with your cast is a valuable approach because it empowers your characters to make their own decisions. It also makes it possible for new characters to suddenly leap into the tale, characters whose existence might frustrate and puzzle you. And, just like Fynch, they may become important. I know that's confronting if you're a textbook planner but trust your instincts. You're still in charge and have that marvellous delete key if you decide something isn't working.

Fynch stayed and kept growing in stature until I realised the entire story relied upon him. He became pivotal to the plot without any conscious help from me. It was an important lesson I learned early in my career.

NAMING YOUR CHARACTERS

Naming your characters appropriately is critical to the credibility of the world you've set up. It is far more important than it initially sounds. Get it right and no one notices – the reading experience can be smooth as silk but get it wrong and it can damage your story.

I exaggerate once again simply for effect but there's no point in having a barbarian horde in the mountains with names like Tim or Edward. Tim is too small and modern. Edward is lovely but it sounds too English for this use. My barbarians have celtic-sounding names like Lothryn or Cailech.

In my historical fiction, which is often based in and around the Edwardian era or soon after, I have come to realise that there wasn't a massive range of names to choose from. The common man was called William, Hugh, Henry,

John, Matthew or indeed Edward. But I work within this range as it is very important in this genre to get the name historically accurate. It's also important to match the name to the region that person comes from.

Eden Valentine in *The Tailor's Girl* was named first and foremost because both names work in a delicious, lyrical harmony. They also in fit beautifully with someone who designs and creates exquisite garments. We get to know Eden on the brink of the roaring twenties in London so her surname needed to work in the Savile Row tailoring circles of that era. Research showed that Valentine is not only a very old name in England but that it works as a Jewish name too.

Your character's name really must work hard to fit her as snugly as possible. I sometimes change a name several times until I find the one that sits with ease on the character and her emerging personality. The name Claire Nightingale, who is a lead character in *Nightingale*, would not suit Stella Myles in *The Last Dance*.

In *The Lavender Keeper*, Lisette Forester in English became Lisette Forrestier in French and also worked back against German for her role as a French woman, with German parentage, living as a spy in occupied France. I went back and forth with several surnames until this one seemed to sit on her well.

Jamie Wren in *Nightingale* and Alex Wynter in *The Tailor's Girl* wear their names so comfortably that, even though they were the first names that arrived into my mind, it never occurred to me to change them.

It's fun finding the right names for your characters, so enjoy the process. Try not to stress about it. The right names will, in the end, find you if you don't hold the reins too tight. Remain open to changing names until you feel that hum of pleasure that signifies the ideal name has arrived: a name that suits the story, suits the world, suits its era and, especially, suits the person attached to it.

Finding a solid rhythm to the name is another aspect I focus on. It's a little anal to think this way, I agree, but I think rhythm is everything in writing. For me, there's a rhythm to be found in each name of each character, just as there is a rhythm to various aspects of the novel. I discuss rhythm in more depth in the chapter 'Rhythm, Pace and Structure'.

There is a propensity among the fantasy writing community to use difficult names and I just don't get it. Why load up names with apostrophes, hyphens and odd sounding syllables that only serve to confuse and irritate your reader? There's nothing clever about this. Yes, it sounds otherworldly but it can work against you. It can rip your enamoured reader out of that lovely bubble where she has suspended her disbelief and dump her back into reality as she frowns and tries to get her mind around how to pronounce the complex name before her. In the end she gives up and makes a phonetic sound in her mind that's vaguely comparable to the letters she can see.

If, after taking years to perfect your manuscript, you come up with a name like D'Aranverenz'gork-Al-Roy, son of

B'Egervoganz'gork-Al-Vey – okay, I'm exaggerating! – the reader will quite possibly end up with something along the lines of 'Dergork son of Begork' in her mind. The reader can't be bothered to labour on the name and substitutes something convenient.

It'd be a real pity if your names were to dissuade an editor from acquiring your manuscript. At best they'd suggest that you reconsider names because the proofing process alone would be a nightmare.

For those who love outlandish names, why make it easy for a commissioning editor to turn away from your novel and say no?

Why not make it as easy as possible for an editor to say yes? That's my mantra and something that I repeat to every writer that I meet. Make it easy for every reader, including every editor, to say yes!

And I have that approach to the editing process. Be easy. You're trying to get noticed, you're trying to win the support and backing of a major commercial organisation for your novel that means everything to you. Don't make it hard for them to love you or love your work. We'll talk about this more in the closing chapter.

Back to naming and, by extension, language in general. You will never appeal to the mainstream reader – or even the casual fantasy or sci-fi reader – if you make them feel inadequate when they pick up your book. It's no good saying you don't care about those readers. You should care – their book-buying decisions have the potential to

put your children through school and win you new contracts. You will not make money from the tiny horde or
readers who want to keep fantasy cultish. If you want to
be the next George R R Martin, make sure you care about
readers who are not necessarily fantasy nuts, the readers
who are ill-prepared for names like Lord H'ordaran de se
Fara'Meerson. This is loony, as far as I'm concerned – call
him Lord Hordaran and be done with it.

In Percheron, I picked names with Zs and Qs to make
them look exotic but I kept them simple and phonetic. So
we have characters called Lazar, Boaz, Herezah and Tariq.
They're not especially difficult to pronounce but with that
single Z or Q they promote the right atmosphere. When
they're used in context the world sounds instantly exotic
and conjures that ambience of a medieval Arabic place.

I do believe it's in the detail that you win. Other writers
probably can't understand what I'm fussing about but then,
I always have the mass market in mind. I want as many
readers as possible to topple into my stories helplessly and
then not be able to put them down. You should want the
same if you're reading this book.

CHARACTER PERSPECTIVE

Every character has a different story to tell; they each see
the world from a different perspective.

Imagine the scene of a car accident with half-a-dozen
witnesses. They may all give roughly the same story but

each will tell it differently: each will have noticed different aspects and each will have different understandings about what happened and why.

It's no different for your story.

Before you set out, be confident in whose story you're telling and why. You don't have to tell the story of just one character, of course. If you take the third-person perspective, then you can show the story through various characters and their perspectives. It's really only when you go into first person that you begin to limit yourself to being able to show only what your narrator can see, hear, experience.

If you're a new writer and you don't feel confident to show the story entirely through the perspective of one narrator, which some writers just naturally can do – and I admire – then my suggestion is you work with the third-person omnipotent perspective so you can range from character to character and allow the reader to be all-seeing, all-hearing in terms of what everyone in your cast it up to.

7.

DIALOGUE

Writing dialogue terrified me when I was first setting out. I thought I knew how people spoke but putting it onto the page threw it into a new dimension – a strange and clumsy one. If you write down how we speak, and I mean exactly how we speak, it's awful. We um, we aah, we have long pauses but we also talk over one another – especially when we're excited – and we cut each other off. This is just how conversations go. I commit the crime of finishing other people's sentences if they are slow speakers. I don't mean to do it but I am hideously impatient. We're also repetitive, especially when we're making a point, and, sadly, often we don't make a point at all! Plus we make whole sentences from one word, for example 'Absolutely!' and 'Awesome!' which we then say rather often and while this seems to flow in real life, on paper it doesn't work.

So, while trying to make their characters sound authentic, the writer of commercial fiction has to cut away all the unnecessary jabber that we hear in real-life conversation.

Keep these points in mind when crafting your dialogue:

- *Dialogue needs to pop from the page.* Imagine cooking popcorn and that delicious sound as the kernels explode beneath the lid of your saucepan. That's how dialogue should feel: full of motion, exploding off the page to make the character come alive in the mind of your reader.
- *Dialogue should be crisp and spare.* Encourage your characters to say as much as possible in as few words as possible. Less is always more.
- *Dialogue must be relevant.* If what each character is saying isn't pushing the story forward, or imparting some vital piece of exposition, then delete it. By exposition in dialogue I mean it should be revealing some aspect of the character or plot. Be disciplined about what your cast is saying – no unnecessary jabber, please.

Each of the individual voices in your tale must be heard. They should be recognisable and they should sound rich and real in the mind of the reader. By rich, I mean spiced by each character's personality – a personality that you have beautifully passed on to the reader without them actually knowing it.

If you rely on your characters to explain what's going

on in the story using their decisions, their actions and their dialogue, then you can never be accused of anything but permitting your readers to experience the story. The most sparkling aspect of dialogue is that it is all showing and no telling.

DIALOGUE IS NOT ALWAYS VERBAL

Body language conveys its own information and you should be highly aware of using people's mannerisms, gestures and facial expressions to convey more than what they're saying. In fact, body language can be used to convey the opposite of what your character is saying. It is a secret language of sorts but one that is visible if you know where to look. Your reader, if you let them, will pick up plenty from what you're showing in terms of character gesture.

Let's look at an example.

'You know I love you' is an overused phrase but let's use it. Its meaning seems obvious.

Look what happens when you add some action or body language.

'You know I love you,' she said, her tone mocking.

'You know I love you,' he said, unable to meet her gaze.

'You know I love you,' she said, and leapt from the balcony.

'You know I love you,' he said, reaching for the knife.

Then you can take away the verbal clues and leave the reader with only the body language.

> Her mind felt dulled from the small talk. Her attention wandered and was arrested by the loudness of a man's tie at the back of the room. Her gaze lifted to meet his and he surprised her with a wink. He'd clearly been watching, waiting for her to seek him out. Blushing, she forced her mind back to the quartet she was standing with. The conversation had moved into deeper tedium. Her treacherous gaze cut his way. He was still staring at her and now he smiled.

Here we're giving the reader a glimpse into these characters' personalities without any dialogue being exchanged and yet they're still communicating.

THE VALUE OF INTERNAL DIALOGUE

Finally, there's the internal dialogue of characters that is a powerful method to convey information to your reader. I use it frequently. I let the reader in on what the character is thinking as a means of keeping the plot rolling forward at that lovely, brisk clip that commercial fiction needs.

He said and *she said* is just fine, by the way. We are so trained to see these neutral qualifiers that they have a magical knack of disappearing from our vision. What we do notice is when the author starts to get overly creative with qualifiers. He shouted, she screamed, he growled, she sighed, he exclaimed, she sneered, he spat and she hissed and so on.

Now I like to use a few of these, everyone does, but it's wise to be aware of when you're using them. Make sure that they are employed only when it's important to portray mood or tone. They're wearying if used too often.

Defer to the he said/she said combo or, if your dialogue is up to the challenge, scrap them all together. It may not even need them.

Feel like a dialogue exercise?

Exercise

- Write some dialogue between two people. Let's have a woman opening the front door to a man who has knocked on it to ask a question about whether someone is at home. Keep it simple, allow for about four or five exchanges between them.
- Now, use the same exchanges, except this time have the woman aged eighty-nine and have the man as a teenager.
- Do it again, this time cast the female as a teenager and the male as a boy aged ten.
- Do it again. The woman is twenty-eight and gorgeous. The man knocking on the door is a thirty-year-old tradie.

- Again, this time the woman is a new mother. The man knocking on the door is a fifty-something official.
- How about this one: the female answering is a little girl. The man at the door is a bikie.
- One last time. The woman answering is senior but not elderly. She's hard of hearing. The man at the door is twenty, selling something.

Are you feeling the difference in how each person talks? Do you think your reader could guess at who these people are just from the dialogue? Could your reader tell their age? If not, you have to work harder to convey the information.

Now let's ramp up that exercise.

- Let's have two people talking. Choose one of the above pairs of people.
- Re-work the dialogue, this time adding body language.
- Add in internal dialogue.

Show these characters in conversation, in motion.

8.

EXPOSITION

When I first set out, understanding exposition was a bit of grey area in storytelling for me, so let's define this, shall we?

Exposition sets the stage for your story. It provides the reader with:

- A sense of the theme, for example a story of betrayal and revenge.
- The world in which it's set, for example Northern Europe.
- The era, for example Paris in 1900.
- The background to the characters, such as their motivations, secrets, upbringing, desires and passions.
- The circumstances by which we find ourselves at this point; in other words, what has just happened?

- The mood of the situation we're being thrown into.
  For instance, let's say we arrive into an argument.
  Is it angry or are the characters just niggling
  one another? Is it a storm in a teacup, a tiff, a
  disagreement; is it playful or bitter, confident or
  hesitant? What's the mood of the scene?

Exposition is the important background information that is *necessary* for the reader to understand what is occurring in the plot.

Please note the word necessary. Too often irrelevant exposition is piled into a manuscript.

EXPOSITION TRAPS

Exposition is vital. However, the danger for new writers is presenting too much background at once – this is called an information dump. It pays to be aware of whether your audience is ready to learn the background information. They may not care about a particular character yet, or you might be overloading them with information about an aspect of the story that isn't relevant.

Bad exposition occurs in two ways. First there's the 'idiot lecture', which starts along the lines of, 'As you know, John, I think . . .' Suddenly we have characters explaining stuff to each other that the reader gleans both should already know. And it becomes obvious that it's amateurish show-casing of detail purely for the observer i.e. the reader. You don't want this happening anywhere in your manuscript.

There's an equally dangerous exposition trap for new writers of giving too much information because they know something about the topic. It might be music, it might be dance, it might be knitting or dog training. I'm not saying don't impart information, I'm suggesting that you keep your audience in mind. The majority of your readers don't care nearly as much as you do. It's very easy to overdo if it's a subject close to your heart. Let's say you know about flying an aeroplane. It's your hobby, you've done all the training, you've got all the hours up, you've even mortgaged yourself to the hilt to own a half-share in a light aircraft and this hobby brings you tremendous joy. You will not be able to help introducing flight into your novel and you may not be able to help putting a pilot into the story.

At this point there's absolutely nothing wrong with this. In fact, how excellent that when you write the flying scene you really do understand all the practicalities, all the checks and safety measures, all the sequences that the pilot will go through and the systems and skills that are employed to not only get the plane off the ground but to keep it airborne.

This know-how is an impeccable tool – that is, until you take that tool and start beating the reader over the head with it and overloading them with detail.

This is when the author comes pushing through and the reader can hear a voice overriding what she's reading and that voice is saying 'I know all of this. I am an expert. Aren't

I impressive? I not only write books but I fly planes. I took years to learn, so now you're going to appreciate how much effort it took to learn to fly while I raised my family and worked full-time and dreamed about writing a book.'

This is an easy trap to fall into. Just like badly handled narrative, clumsily handled exposition can quickly bore the reader because they don't care about any of the background you're giving because they haven't yet invested in the plot. And what is it that makes the plot? Character, yes! So if you haven't made us care about the characters, then we don't give a flying fig about your exposition.

HOW TO HANDLE EXPOSITION

First you have to make us *care* about your characters and their conflict before you start threading in your exposition.

And you have to make us curious about the situation that the lead characters find themselves in when we meet them. Plus, you need to capture our imagination for the world you've thrown us into whether it's deep space, medieval Europe, Victorian England or contemporary rural Australia.

Once your characters have entered our hearts and we're beginning that delicious surrender to your storytelling, then you can start to introduce details that'll help us understand the story and its cast.

Exposition is a tricky skill to master, it takes time and a lot of practice.

Dialogue and exposition

Here's an example of badly handled exposition in eighty-four words:

> John was angry about today's meeting and how James had trampled everyone seated around the boardroom table. He was so fed up in fact that he poured himself a slug of scotch – and he didn't even like scotch. It was a malt, not meant to be gobbled and so it burned all the way down. But it didn't change his mood. John was still fuming. But at least he had his beautiful wife, Sarah, waiting at home for him. She could always soothe him.

That's a lot of *awful* telling and no showing. It's an amateurish way to convey exposition.

Let's recast this same scene but this time going straight into dialogue. It's barely twice as long but is more adept storytelling and the exposition is threaded through the scene so you learn as the action moves forwards.

> 'Wow, you look angry,' Sarah remarked as John arrived home and gave her a perfunctory kiss. 'Drink?' she said, moving to the kitchen bench. 'This ten-year-old malt sample came in from one of our best distilleries.' She brandished a bottle glowing with amber liquid. 'I know you don't like whiskey but . . .'

'Open the damn scotch,' John sighed, flinging down the briefcase.

'Careful,' she admonished in a gentle tone, crystal catching the same light that her dark eyes reflected as she offered the glass. 'I saved for that briefcase so you'd look like a real lawyer on your first day.' She pecked him tenderly, mellow fumes of the liquor scenting the space she left as she withdrew. 'You've already survived six years with James.'

John ran a hand through his tobacco-coloured hair in a gesture of resignation. 'He was such a bastard in the boardroom. Talked over everyone, listened to none of us and said no to all the proposals.' She watched him drain the slug of malt in one swallow. 'That burns.' Sarah noted his voice had already softened to its pillow tenderness.

'Still angry?'

'Yes, but not with you. Never with you.'

The second example was all about showing not telling. We learned so much:

- John had a meeting today.
- John doesn't usually drink whiskey but he's angry enough to do just that.
- We know why he's angry and who he's angry with.
- John's partner is Sarah.
- We get the impression that Sarah loves him because she saved so hard to give him the leather briefcase.

We also sense that he loves her back because, angry as he is, he doesn't take it out on her.

- John is a lawyer.
- He's worked at the firm for six years, surviving James.
- We know Sarah works and that she has something to do with the liquor industry.
- We get the impression that she knows how to handle John when he's stressed.
- We get an impression of their age.

The scene has action, movement and some background shadings of where this scene is taking place. It includes a lot of exposition in a very brief exchange while also letting the reader into the lives and personality of two characters. We learn far more than in the first instance with a greater sense of story and in only twice as many words.

Keep it relevant

Unless it's important for the reader to know a fact, in order for them to understand the story, don't include it. For instance, if the fact that a character likes to wear extremely loud ties works as a glimpse into his extroverted nature, then share it. If it doesn't colour in part of his personality or give us some vital clue in the story, then it's unnecessary storytelling clutter.

Be brutal. Remember the pilot anecdote. Knowing about 'stuff' is a brilliant boon to your writing but knowing what to leave out is a skill. Acquire it!

Always aim for a light touch with exposition

By this I mean less is more. Your story will become robust if you learn to weave the exposition through the narrative. I've already touched on this and will talk in more detail about it in the coming chapter but, because it's so important, I'll reiterate: exposition needs to be shown, and it's best shown through dialogue.

Go back to your favourite three bestselling writers in your chosen genre.

Read them again and analyse how they thread important information that the reader needs to know through their narrative, never letting it run for too long. More importantly, notice how they drip-feed exposition through the dialogue i.e. the vital clues to the backstory or to a character and their motivations.

Showing not telling is a subtle skill, and one of the hardest-acquired ones for commercial writing.

For an aspiring writer, keep this in mind: if you handle your exposition well and the commissioning editor is barely aware of your providing her with all the information she needs to know to understand the story, then it's a huge leap and a massive subconscious tick when she's appraising your manuscript.

If the information is important to the story and necessary for its atmosphere, or if it's vital for us to grasp something so as to access a character's personality, then you need to have a light touch when passing this knowledge onto us as your audience.

Checklist

Exposition needs to be:

- Relevant. Can the reader get on without it? Ask yourself this all the time.
- Drip-fed through dialogue.
- Woven into the story's narrative.
- Shown through the actions and decisions of your characters.

9.

DIGGING DEEP

Beyond a good story achieved through excellent characterisation, there are two key aspects to your writing that a commissioning editor will be looking for. The first is particularly necessary for anyone who is hoping to tap into the juggernaut that is women's fiction.

Is it an emotional read? Does it make the reader laugh or cry – perhaps both? Does it provoke thoughts of past romantic relationships or does it make them hungry for one? Does it make the reader sad or angry? Can the reader touch the bitterness of the character and as a result be able to see behind it and understand what makes the character tick?

The question is about being able to inject emotion – be in tension, anger, sorrow, joy – into your story through your characters and, just as importantly, it's about injecting emotion into the atmosphere of your scenes.

Emotion should become a major cornerstone of your writing, one that a commissioning editor and indeed a reader will be looking for.

The second aspect is that old chestnut that I keep referring to.

Is this writer showing me the story rather than telling me the story? I know I risk boring you by referring to it again but this is a tough concept to grasp. I am convinced that every novelist grapples with it. I certainly wrestle with it every day that I write. Am I showing? It is like a parrot that sits on my shoulder and squawks, 'Or is that telling?' in my ear.

My mantra is: am I allowing the reader to experience this scene, or are they acquiring dry information from the page?

If you accept that this is without doubt the trickiest part of writing a novel, then how are you going to show and not tell?

ENGAGING THE SENSES

The best way you can show and not tell is by engaging the senses of your reader.

We've already talked about dialogue as a failsafe method of showing and not telling, so long as it doesn't fall into the idiot lecture or info-dump type of dialogue.

Let's now talk about the stuff beyond your characters'

voices and how you evoke the world. Let's drill it down further. How do you evoke each scene without telling but showing and how, at the same time, do you tap into the emotion of your reader and get them to surrender to the read with their imagination and their own emotional response?

First, please accept that your reader is your partner. A book is a partnership. It's a handshake between writer and reader. You promise to deliver a brilliant story that will keep your reader happily turning the pages. The reader promises to bring all their life experiences, imagination and emotion and lay them bare to your story. The reader must *surrender*. It's a very personal pact that you make to one another. And for the read to be successful, both must deliver on their promise.

So how do you tap into all that the reader has promised you: her life's experiences, her imagination, her emotions?

You do that by engaging the five senses that you possess, that your reader possesses and of course that your characters possess. Incidentally, in fantasy we can move into the sixth sense, which we call Wit. For example we may have magical mindlink for dialogue or we may have alien characters that don't possess the same senses.

In a recent writing masterclass of mine we came up with a new sense that impressed me. This cohort identified Perception as a sense. I have to agree. Some people are more perceptive than others and it's an inherent part of your make-up in terms of how fast or deeply you pick up on an atmosphere in a room, or the dynamics between a group of people and so on. I was most impressed by this fantastic notion and congratulations to that group of fine writers – you know who you are.

Going back to strictly human senses and their emotions, it's those that you must engage if you want your reader to surrender to your story. By surrendering to the story they become one of the characters – your reader *is* your invisible character and you must never, never ignore them.

EVOKING EMOTION

I won't say anything more important than this in all the pages I've written in this guide: as a writer of popular fiction your whole reason for being is to *release* in your readers an emotional response to your storytelling. If you can't tap into your readers' emotions, you will seriously struggle to win a publisher's attention. They don't tell you this, but I will: if your writing doesn't promote an emotional response, *it will not sell*.

An injection of brief but evocative descriptions will lift your storytelling out of the pages and into the minds of the readers. Your aim through description is to allow your reader to picture themselves in that scene as well, walking alongside your characters.

Are you comfortable with the concept that in order to write good commercial fiction, you have to win an emotional investment from your readers in the same way that music wins an emotional response from a listener or a movie can make you cry?

As a writer, you are the trigger. Your words, the images they evoke, the experiences they evoke in the readers' minds unleash the imagination of the readers and fling them into the world of your story.

The five human senses – along with wit and perception – are vital to your storytelling and newer writers don't realise how powerful they are until they lock onto them.

Exercise

Try this:
- Picture yourself travelling alone on a long flight.
- Write down everything you can possibly think of that you can hear.
- Now do the same for the other four senses.

Have you only recorded the obvious? If you think you have, go deeper. Close your eyes and let go, remember every detail you can about your last long-haul flight.

You might be surprised by the amount of sensory information you've come up with while you're sitting at home and imagining yourself on a plane. And if you can imagine it, so can your reader. Most of your readers will have taken a long flight. What you must do is tap into their memory and emotional recollections of their in-flight experiences.

All you have to do is pick out a few of these aspects and your scene will come to life. Be careful not to be too obvious – they can do the obvious themselves.

You should start noticing the kid kicking you in the back, or the smell of the attendant's perfume when she leans across to hand you your tray. Perhaps you then wonder how she gets to look so groomed: she's travelled the same distance and you look like hell. How about how the blanket feels against your skin, or what the air conditioning on board sounds like?

Instantly your reader has the image in mind and they're beginning to 'experience' the setting. Then off you go – you've imprinted the scene on the reader and now it's time to get on with the dialogue and the story.

It's important that you don't labour the five senses – they're a subtle tool so use them sparingly but frequently. If you overload it, you'll end up overwriting the scene, which won't do you any favours.

Rich detail that evokes the picture is everything you are aiming for in your descriptions.

- Richness of detail achieves the sense of place and time that publishers want.
- Sensory detail that evokes an emotional response is showing and not telling.
- Evoking emotion will win you attention from a potential editor.

And, dear writer, you must now focus on achieving this for every scene that you craft. No character is walking around in a vacuum and no two characters involved in any sort of conversation are exchanging dialogue in a void, either. Stuff is happening around them, they are gesturing and they are moving, even if it's a simple blink, or a touch of the hair. This is your story in motion. This is your story being experienced.

You must also make sure that each scene feels real, that you are keeping the reader in the moment of the unfolding conversation, by setting that scene and then constantly adjusting it and layering in more information. This technique will also push the story forward and give the reader all the important clues.

AUTHENTICITY

Let's ramp up the sensory experience of the novel and emotional response for the reader.

I go to just about all the locations in my novels so I've already immersed my five senses in these places, whether it's an old bookshop in Paris or an ancient gaol in the Tower of London. I've touched, smelled, tasted, listened, seen – and I bring all of that to my books.

I'm doing the double whammy. Not only am I dreaming up sensory information so that my reader, too, can employ their imagination, but I am also giving them factual sensory information that I have gleaned from my travels – no imagination, all truth and that's what really brings the book to life.

Not every writer can visit the locations of their novel, nor might they want to. I do because it's second nature to me – I have been travelling all of my life and have been fortunate to see a lot of the world. I am prepared to invest earnings in travel for my books because all of my books have an international flavour. Plus I'm particularly passionate about evoking a strong sense of place with the right images for my reader.

I love having my readers involved in armchair travel with me. But I accept not everyone feels the same away about their storytelling – we are all wired differently. I enjoy immersing myself in a location, so it's an education and enrichment for me long before it finds its way into a book.

I argue, though, that when it does find its way in, the authenticity of my locations is there. No doubt this is why so many readers have a strong sense of place when reading my stories.

For those who cannot travel, or choose not to put their feet on the ground of where their stories are set, I shall offer a gentle warning in recommending that you do not write about Cairo or Istanbul, for instance, if you don't know what those cities look like, feel like, smell like, taste like and sound like.

You'll be quickly found out because today we are all great travellers, and the chances of your reader having already visited your location are high. If you must write about, say, Paris and have never set your big toe on a Parisian foot-path, then be sure to do your research. Readers demand authenticity. I suggest you don't acquire your knowledge from the single perspective of Wikipedia.

You can't make everything up. Your story is out of your imagination but if you're setting your characters down in Adelaide then you need to know the area and be accurate about where the mall is and where a coffee shop or bar is located. You should have a good idea of what the architecture of your setting looks and feels like. This is you as the writer paying your dues. When I was writing my two DCI Jack Hawksworth crime books – *Bye Bye Baby* and *Beautiful Death* – I took my research to the nth degree by visiting the London pub I was to have him drinking in. I made sure I had the right beer on tap and that I knew the menu he would order from, where he'd sit, what that corner felt like, where the light fell and so on. Now, some of you may think this is extreme and that's fine, but you won't earn the respect of your readers if you don't do some research and strive for authenticity.

If you don't want to visit or don't have the funds to visit your overseas location, I would go so far as to recommend that you don't include it. If you do include a location without knowing the region firsthand then be prepared to take some flak from those who do if you get any aspect inaccurate.

Fantasy writers, you have lots more leeway because you are designing your worlds and can manipulate your settings to suit. However, you too have an obligation to keep your world authentic.

It doesn't matter what you're writing, here's a helpful list of subjects to keep in mind when you are building the bubble of your world around your reader:

- Culture
- Spirituality and religion
- Politics
- Recent and ancient history
- Architecture
- Music, art, entertainment
- Folklore
- Mixture of cultures
- Social structure
- Work, the labour force and industry
- Farming and agriculture
- Technology
- Government
- Education
- Lifestyles
- Hobbies, pastimes and sports
- Food
- Fashion
- Transport
- Landscape.

I could go on but hopefully you get my drift.

Know your world. Know your setting and how people respond to it in order to evoke the right images in your readers' minds or to tap into their familiarity with that place. If you're writing fantasy, then you must present your world fully formed and in rich detail so the reader can build it quickly around the story.

RESEARCH

I've told you that I'm a gunslinger in every sense when it comes to crafting my novels. I'm frankly embarrassed by how little planning goes into any aspect of them and I am always privately surprised that I end up with a story that makes any sense at all. However, I don't question the universe on this and I never analyse my quirky approach. If I can use a well-worn phrase – it's just how I'm wired. Nevertheless, in spite of all that gun-slinging, there is one area of the building of my novel that I am far more focused on than any other and that's my research. I don't plan it, I don't necessarily have a list I have to tick off but it's as though I open a file in my mind of 'stuff' I must pay attention to.

Research for a novel is where some very hard yards will be run – often frustrating yards. I put a great deal of effort into this area of my work and while there is little that is especially organised about it – for instance, 'Ian, I have to get to the Imperial War Museum and soak up some knowledge,' it really is as vague as that – I don't set off on my novel's journey without immersing myself as best I can into its era and the events I think I might need.

So I'm warning you now if you're hoping to swim in

the big pond where all the big fish play, you need to understand that most authors are paying attention to sense of place, sense of era, sense of colour and atmosphere and they achieve this by paying their dues at the time of researching for their novel.

How long do candles burn? How much was a pint of beer in 1910? When was a town or village electrified?

Sense of place, the authenticity, will be greatly helped by your five senses. For anyone doing period manuscripts, you have a big job ahead of you in ensuring your research is spot on.

Look beyond your characters and see what's around them. This will help you to add all the shadings and textures that the editor is searching for to convince her she's not only in a period story but she's in the right period. If you contradict the details, you risk losing her. It's a dead giveaway if you have glass when glass was not commonly used or gas lighting before gas lighting was commonplace.

Getting the right vehicles on the roads is paramount. I have spent days and days just drilling down to find an appropriate car for 1919 – so I knew where it was made, how it was made, what its inside looked like and how it worked.

It's really no good getting everything right – down to the kind of bonnet a woman was wearing – and then having the wrong sort of horse and carriage trundling along.

If you don't know, *don't make it up*. Find out. There are always readers out there who know something about the period you're writing in, or the subject you're writing about, or the historical event to which you refer and will take much glee in pointing out your failing if you've got a fact wrong.

Research is the burden of writing historical – it means you are going to be trawling websites and reading, reading, reading loads of reference material. I spend thousands of dollars on reference books. I have them all lined up and ready to go before I embark on each novel. Some of them are highly general in nature. If I'm freefalling into my story and need to know about the hemline of women's skirts in the winter of 1919 in southern England, I can work it out quickly from my history-of-fashion bible. But then I have dedicated history books. In *Nightingale*, for example, in my tower of bedside books was a history of Gallipoli based entirely on the Ottoman campaign rather than the ANZAC campaign. I needed to understand the Turkish perspective, timing of Turkish movements, placement of troops, training, even food rations.

As I've said we're not all wired the same way, so what works for me won't necessarily feel ideal for you. However, just to give you an insight, let me tell you how I prepare for a new novel. To start, I am usually working on the research at least one year out.

Today is 14 December. It's a Sunday. I have recently finished a five-state book tour and in fact am still in promotional mode for one particular novel and will continue for the next month or two. While that book tour has been underway I have arranged my travel and media schedule so that I can work on the copyedit of a new novel that is due to publish in less than four months. I finished finessing the final chapter in the early hours of this morning. Between the current book tour and the copyedit for my next novel, I have also been writing – when I can – a new novel that will be published next Christmas. I am only 20 000 words into it but it is moving. Soon I will focus almost exclusively on that book – it will be an intensive couple of months up until its delivery date. *But* while all of this is raging, I am also reading books around the topic of the novel that will follow in two years' time. The books have begun arriving from all over the world and form my before-bed reading. People are often surprised that I don't read much fiction but that's because I mostly stick to nonfiction for my novel research. Regardless, I'm never not reading – I'm never without a book. I'm about to take a four-hour flight and I'm carrying a big book about the history of the French country house to read while I'm in the air.

For each book I now have at least, and I do mean *at least*, a dozen historical tomes to teach me what I need to know about any given period.

For *The Lavender Keeper* I had to learn not only about the period of World War Two but also the various theatres of war that were going on. It wasn't a simple war, there were fronts – there were fronts in France, Italy, North Africa and Eastern Europe and each had its own atmosphere, flavours, scenes, equipment, needs and pressures.

I had to learn all about Hitler. I needed to understand a lot more about his policies and and what drove them, about the political climate in Germany and greater Europe that permitted Hitler's ascendance. I needed to get a handle on the Nazi hierarchy and soon realised I was getting down to tiny detail such as knowing about the Nazi uniforms, too, including specifics such as the different buttons they wore, because I had a scene where a Nazi colonel and his lover undo those buttons. It suddenly became vitally important that I knew exactly what a Nazi colonel in 1943 was wearing. Close enough just wasn't good enough.

No matter what genre you are writing, if you want to be at the top of your game, then don't guess!

In writing *The Lavender Keeper*, I also had to know what people were eating in 1942. Not just in London, either. I had to know what they were eating in Paris and what they were eating in rural France. There are a host of regional dishes in southern France so I really did have to ensure I got it right.

I had to learn all about lavender, too. Not just modern-day lavender farming but back prior to the war. How was it grown, where was it grown and in what quantities? How was it reaped and with what? Who harvested it? How was it stored and what happened next? How was the oil extracted? What was lavender oil used for and why? Why did the Germans want it?

Fast forward to 1950s, the setting of *The Lavender Keeper* sequel *The French Promise*. How was oil gathered then and how was it extracted?

What about the Holocaust? Oh my goodness, that was an enormous subject to learn about and a responsibility that couldn't be taken lightly because the emotional side to that research was daunting and confronting. I was able to move readers during the prologue of *The French Promise* because I had been to Auschwitz and experienced its horror that echoes so viscerally down the decades, so I was able to convey that horror to my readers. Of course I also read so much about Auschwitz. I immersed my senses in the locales and firsthand interviews from the time so that I could impart the highly emotional atmosphere to the reader.

My travels for these books took me across Europe and, ultimately, to Launceston. I read book after book after book. I watched documentaries. I interviewed dozens of people throughout France, Poland and Australia. I found experts in everything from spy-catching in World War Two to how to blow up a railway line. I not only learned which ships were plying the waters for line voyages between Australia and Britain but also which particular ship would suit my couple at the time that they travelled. Finding that ship took ages.

I learned about lighthouse-keeping and all about the Festival of Britain in 1951 that took over the country. Then after learning about lighthouse-keeping we cut almost all of those scenes. On reflection I see that none of it was wasted because I had a better understanding of my character's tasks, but it was a lot of work for the few lines that clung on in the final version. I looked at Paris in the 1960s and how it had changed, for example from the Nazi occupation of a noble's palace and then its conversion back to a grand house or hotel. How had Provence been affected by its change from sleepy southern town to new tourist destination in the 1960s?

I am not telling you this to boast, impress or daunt you. I am simply giving you the facts about what I had to do to deliver a satisfying duet of books that were rich in their sense of place and era.

And the fact that they both became Penguin's #1 fiction title is testimony to the research.

It is the sense of place, the richness of the landscapes and the history that I've brought back to life that works in concert with a ripping story.

For anyone writing stories set in the past, you should take all this on board because the top historical writers are investing a great deal of time, money and energy in their research.

Contemporary writers are not off the hook either. Whatever genre you're writing, know that the successful authors focus a vast amount of their attention on achieving sense of place, on ensuring an emotional response, and on doing the research hard yards, just as I did for my crime novels. It would be unwise to think you can get away with writing a contemporary story set in Sydney when you last visited it ten years back. It's a different city now with a different vibe and a new generation roaring around it. Go and visit it, understand how it ticks now.

The internet can only teach you so much.

YOUR NOVEL'S WORLD

The setting of your story is another character. Use that character, make it work hard for your readers. In contemporary fiction, stories that are set in London, for example, can just as easily work in Paris or New York but if London and its icons become a part of the fabric of the story, then the world that the author evokes becomes another character. Nowhere is this more relevant than in the worlds that writers build – often from the ground up – for their speculative fiction stories.

It's worth keeping in mind that your reader is never going to love your world as much as you do. While a new make-believe world can be an amazing achievement it is not paramount to a successful speculative fiction story. In other words a popular story can function very successfully in a world we recognise and its only difference will be the existence of magic. Readers are more than willing to come along with me on an epic half-million-word tale knowing ahead that I am not going to give them some extraordinarily new and fascinating world to get to know.

So, what are they going to get with me? Well, apart from great characters and an addictive story – which is where I do tend to hang my hat – they will get a world that feels vaguely strange yet enormously familiar. Most of all it will feel credible. They will get a world where strange creatures abound and where magic is always possible – and those creatures and that magic feel plausible and right among a highly recognisable setting that could be medieval Europe or Ottoman Constantinople.

Be prepared to work hard on this. It's not in the dreaming up of a fabulously exotic world with strange beasts and rivers that run uphill. It's about delivering a world that your reader slips effortlessly into and accepts immediately without question, without frowning, without any loss of impetus for their reading. That is where the real secret to credible world building begins. If you get this bit right, every reader will unconsciously accept your world. Get it wrong and you risk their disappointment.

Let me explain how this works.

It's Sunday. A reader, let's use a working mum as an example, has done her household chores that she needed to get done before the working week begins. The husband's out with the kids leaving her with a rare afternoon off. A meal is in the oven or perhaps they've decided to get takeaway later. The groceries are done – she knows she's got fresh food in the fridge for breakfast and lunch boxes tomorrow morning. And, best of all, the house is quiet. This is her time. She makes a pot of tea or perhaps brews some real coffee as a treat. She may even open that packet of biscuits she's been denying herself or crack into that Easter egg she hid from the kids.

Either way she's now kicking off her shoes and leaning back into the sofa, getting comfy. She picks up the brand-new book that she's been looking forward to – it's by a new author she's taking a chance on. She bought it because she likes the front cover, the blurb and, from the first paragraph or two that she read on her quick trip into the bookstore on her lunch break she decided that she liked the writing style and the setting too.

She takes a sip from her cup, a bite from her biscuit and in she goes.

Now, if the book that she's just opened offers her seamless, hassle-free transportation into a new world, whether it is a corporate thriller or a medieval city, then the author is already winning. This working mum on her precious few hours off is going to read either until her eyes ache or the family returns, noisily demanding to know what's for dinner.

But if the author has been clumsy and the book jars the reader or makes her think too hard about the new world she's supposed to understand and accept, then every time she frowns or re-reads a passage to comprehend it better, she is actually being dragged out of the world. It's a world that everyone from writer to editor, to marketing, PR and sales have worked hard to achieve. At every pause or stumble, she's reminded that she's not in the city of Pearlis or Paris but she's in her family sitting room and she can hear the dog barking across the road, someone's lawn mower droning and the noise of traffic from the road.

She is back where she started and all that hard work of yours has been wasted in building around her what I call the bubble of believability – or 'Bob', as I've nicknamed it. You strive for Bob. Your reader wants Bob in her life. Make sure you do everything in your storytelling to keep Bob intact.

10.

RHYTHM, PACE
AND STRUCTURE

UNDERSTANDING RHYTHM AND PACE

Rhythm and pace are shadowy areas because they're invisible. You can't touch them. You can't hear or taste them and you are, most of the time, as unaware of them as you are your own heartbeat or breath – until you focus on them.

When you focus on rhythm or pace, they can become obvious and as reassuring as a pulse. But they're intangible, so they're tricky to discuss. This is not something to worry about. It's quite an anal sort of topic to even mention because many would argue that they take care of themselves if the storytelling is perfected.

This may well be true but I think rhythm applies to more than just 'the rhythm of the book'. What does that actually mean? It's far too vague a comment to help you get a purchase on rhythm. Had you mentioned it to me when I was starting out I know my typical reaction would have been to blow out my cheeks in frustration and remind myself to worry about the writing of the novel first. This isn't bad advice to be giving you – but as your writing confidence grows and as the spotlight on your storytelling begins to illuminate wider, then rhythm is going to be one of those grey, shadowy, murky areas that will become more important to your writing life.

We all want to improve. I want every novel I write to be better than the last. My audience may not see it this way because everyone has their favourites for different reasons but in terms of my technical skill – the skill of bolting together a story – I want each of my productions to improve. I want my descriptions to be just a bit more powerful than in the previous book. Or I want my characters to leap off the page more elegantly or I want the story's drama to be more intense, the sense of place to feel so real that the reader is right there walking alongside my characters and believing them more than ever.

RHYTHM

- *My writing rhythm for crafting of the novel.* This is where your writing equation comes to the fore and keeps your rhythm regular, disciplined, focused. It forces a rhythm onto you and prevents you from being the ten-hours-a-day on one day and one-hour-a-day the next kind of writer. It will keep your writing pace balanced and the rhythm at which you write smooth and controlled. This makes for a happy writer.

- *The internal rhythm of the novel.* Is the story moving along at a brisk clip? You need it to for commercial fiction. You can't have sluggish parts. The story has to remain in motion, relentlessly pushing to the climax and dragging your helpless, completely addicted reader with it.

- *The rhythm at which the reader reads the book.* For example a couple of chapters before bed or in a feast on a long-haul flight.

- *The structural rhythm of the novel.* Chapters of similar size ensure a rhythmic read that the audience tunes in to. Your reader will soon get a feel for how long each chapter is and say to themselves 'I'll snatch one before shutting off the lights' or 'I can grab one while waiting for the kids to come out from school' or 'I can read three chapters over lunch in the park or sipping a coffee at the local café during a work break'. This may not seem important to you right now but at a more advanced stage – like the stage at which I find myself now – it is useful to think about this sort of stuff. I want everything to be smooth, to make it easy for my reader to be drawn into the world of my story.

- I have found that my personal chapter rhythm is roughly 3500 words. Often I'll write a chapter and

realise it's getting up to 7000 words. If I go back
and look over it I can always find a logical place
to break that chapter into two to ensure a happy
reading rhythm.

- *The way each character speaks has a rhythm.* This is
  something that builds itself as you gain confidence
  with the dialogue you write for your characters.
  Their language choice, their way of speaking, their
  tone – it all amounts to a recognisable rhythm
  so that the he said/she said qualifier may in time
  become unnecessary. Don't stress on this but just
  accept that we all speak to our own rhythm in real
  life and so will your characters.

- *The rhythm of the characters' names.* A good rhythm
  to your characters' names will have a subliminal and
  pleasing effect on the reader. Readers won't notice
  it at a conscious level but you're doing yourself a
  disservice if your names sound clunky when spoken
  aloud, or sound clunky in the mind of the reader.
  I cover this in more detail in the previous chapter.
  The names of each person need to roll off the
  tongue in the readers' minds so that they don't
  hesitate or frown or make an odd sound because
  they can't pronounce it. I needed to name a male
  lead in *Tapestry*. He's a character from the early
  Georgian era of 1715. He's part of the landed
  gentry in England. He's like Darcy in a way: born
  into wealth and so possessing of that confidence

and slight arrogance that wealth brings with it, especially in that period. But I wanted him well away from the Hooray Henry kind of name. I ended up with Julius Sackville. It possessed a pleasing rhythm and I believed it made him sound fearless, wealthy and strong willed. It also endowed him with a name resonant of early Georgian England. If I'd called him Julian instead of Julius, the name immediately became a fraction foppish, and I couldn't have that, which is why I went with the Roman-sounding Julius, as though in another life he may well have led a legion.

PACE

My novels tend to read faster the deeper you go into the story. By the final third of the book it's at a full gallop, as though someone yelled 'Charge!' at about Chapter 23.

What I have learned is that the story is not speeding. The characters aren't hurrying. I'm certainly not writing faster because I stick to my dedicated daily word count that doesn't permit me to race. If I analyse it, what's occurring is that the tension is increasing in the story – this happens as the conflict deepens, the drama heightens and the characters are flung into more stress.

You know how when we're under pressure in any situation it feels like everything is moving twice as fast? Well, that's what is happening in the story. Turn the screws tighter on the characters' problems and the story will zoom along faster for your reader; they may even turn the pages more frantically to see what's going to happen. This is everything we want in commercial fiction!

If I were to draw you a picture of what this looks like, it would be this:

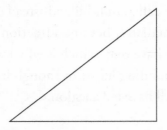

Now, don't glaze over. I promise this isn't to be an arithmetic lesson. Stay with me a moment longer. All I need you to do is note and nod your head that this is indeed a right-angle triangle. Right?

And now if I do this:

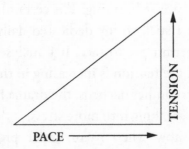

You will see where I'm going with this. The image made a lot of sense to me when Bryce Courtenay originally opened the door to me on this theory.

As you can see, the pace is not changing. It's static. It moves along the same axis. It's the axis of tension that is increasing throughout and the more it increases, the more the reader feels not only heightened drama but a sense of speed at which the story is hurtling along.

Making sense to you? If not, don't worry. It will when you get it out of theory and start the practical business of writing your novel.

Let's keep going with this theory though.

I would love you to accept that this is what a novel looks like. Escalating tension to the point of the climax of the story and then the denouement, or the final scene that pulls together any loose ends or explains what needs to be explained before the characters walk off into the sunset.

For those who learn best with imagery, I'm going to show you the best pictorial explanation possible of what commercial fiction looks like.

Now, stay with me.

If you are happy to accept that this is what a novel looks like pictorially, then I would love it even more if you would go the rest of the way and accept that in commercial fiction, this is how most individual chapters should look. In a perfect world, in a manuscript perfect for commercial fiction, every chapter would have escalating tension. And so would the next.

Okay? Here's the rub. Deep breath.

Each chapter should have a slightly higher level of tension, so your triangle will look a bit taller – because of its greater angle – with each passing chapter.

And – cue triumphant music – when you put it all together, it looks like this:

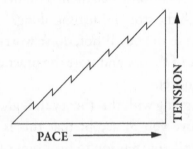

Bryce called this the Sawtooth Method and it made such profound sense to me that day that I wrote my first manuscript with the concept burning so hard in my mind that many people used to say my fantasy books just got faster and faster as they were reading them. *Fab!* I loved hearing this.

These days I don't have to consciously focus on it. My whole writing method and rhythm is attuned to this notion of escalating tension and my stories tend to follow that pattern, which is, at the time of writing, what commercial fiction demands.

Please, don't stress over this. If it makes sense to you and resonates somewhere deep within you as it did for me, then it's going to come. At the outset of your career it's very important you concentrate on character, on showing not telling, on getting your dialogue right and thus getting the story tripping along and expanding with lots of drama.

As you begin to get that part of the recipe of writing commercial fiction bedded down and coming as second nature, all of this more crafty stuff will begin to fall into place. You'll be more aware of it and pay more attention to it but without any angst attached. Please trust yourself.

I should add that I do a whole section on rhythm and pacing in my masterclass but I can't share that here because it requires performance, which in turn draws some perplexed expressions and ultimately some applause. I'm afraid if you want to experience the deep immersion of me performing a book's rhythm and pace, you'll have to come to masterclass!

STRUCTURE

May I make a suggestion to all aspiring writers of commercial fiction? Don't be contemptuous of the traditional storyline with a beginning, middle and end; if you are, then you're significantly reducing your chances of being published. It may sound juvenile, the sort of advice your teacher gave you in Year 7, but, as you'll see, it has genuine merit.

What does the beginning, middle and end of a novel mean?

The whole idea of commercial fiction is that you are building towards something climactic in your story – the focal point of the reader's interest, you might say. Keep in mind that escalating tension we talked about in earlier chapters and imagine it as an ever-tightening skin over the skeleton of your sawtooth novel.

Now, break the story into three.

The *first section* is the beginning of your story. It's where your conflict is laid out, it's where your main characters are introduced, where we understand their prime motivations, what's initially getting in their way and what they plan to do about it. It's here that your reader gets full exposure to the world of your setting and era of your novel as well as its pervading atmosphere.

The *middle section* is the meat of the tale. All the machinations of your various characters are in play here. You are revealing a lot more about all of the characters and their secrets, their decisions are affecting each other and the drama is in full flight. In fact, we learn most of what we need to about the characters and their motivations at this stage.

Subplots are unfolding, secondary characters are becoming more important and a lot of the major action is taking place. Clues to the ultimate outcome of the story are planted. Remember, tension is escalating as per the sawtooth and it feels like the read itself is getting faster towards the end of this middle section.

And the *final section* is the end. It sounds obvious enough but it's here that you punish your leads the most so as to make the reader feel as though your characters are never going to achieve what they set out to do. The conflict should be at its most potent and the drama at its most frantic. Your characters should be running out of time, out of steam, out of ideas, even out of love. Then the epiphany: something momentous spurs your protagonist to dig deep, conquer the fear and find the courage and the energy to face their challenges. It's here that you reward your reader. While the story itself may not have a happy ending, it's in the final chapters that you give the reader a sense of hope. This hope makes the book feel worthwhile and valuable to your reader.

I'm simplifying it. There's the five-part structure as well: exposition, rising action, climax, falling action and denouement but that's making it all sound a bit scientific. It's also suggesting there is a given structure, which there is not. Your novel will have its own plot, its own tension and high points, so really, so long as you can be mindful of having a beginning, middle and end to your story – and pay attention to everything else in the previous pages – I think you'll have a happy editor.

KNOW THE DIFFERENCE BETWEEN THEMES, PLOTS AND STORIES

Theme is often confused with plot and plot is often confused with story. Let's break it down and get clear about the trio.

Theme

Theme can be summarised in a sentence or less. It is a notion or a couple of notions around which the book revolves. Examples might be loss, unrequited love, betrayal, revenge and so on. It's quite handy to know the main themes spicing your story – you can apply it to your synopsis and your blurb writing along with your submissions to publishers and agents.

When you summarise a theme it can sound sombre but that doesn't mean the novel is gloomy. Mine aren't and they're almost always about betrayal or revenge. Remember my previous advice – contented characters make for very dull reading!

Plot

Plot is what happens in your story and why.

Plot grows out of the characters. If you keep your characters in an intriguing situation and in conflict, then one event leads to another and you have a plot.

Plot begins with an idea or a question. For example, what if during World War Two a French resistance fighter from Provence, a British female spy and a German colonel of the Wehrmacht form a tense love triangle that will test their loyalties? This single-sentence idea prompted my novel *The Lavender Keeper* and its sequel.

Story

Story is often confused with plot. Story is the sequence of action that occurs inside the plot, 'this happened then that happened'.

As the novelist E M Forster famously explained in the late 1920s:

> The King died and then the Queen died.

This is story. You can see the facts in sequential order.

> The King died and then the Queen died because of grief.

This is plot. What happened and why? It's the guiding idea.

Here's another way to differentiate:
- Story is the emotional journey of the characters.
- Plot is formed by the decisions of the characters.

And now you know exactly what I'm going to say next. The trick is to balance the two as effortlessly as you can.

Exercise

Here's an exercise to help you identify theme, plot and story.
 I think most of us are aware of the tale of *Cinderella*.
- What are the key themes?
- Can you summarise the *Cinderella* plot in a few main points?
- Can you write down what the story is about in fewer than 200 words?

Did you arrive at something like this?

Themes:
Poverty and wealth; love and abandonment; good and evil.

Plot points:
- Cinderella is forbidden to attend the royal ball.
- A fairy godmother magically arrives to dress Cinderella and have her taken to the ball. But she must leave before the stroke of midnight.
- Cinderella and the Prince fall in love and at midnight she runs from the palace but loses one of her slippers in her haste.
- The Prince uses the glass slipper to find his beloved; although every spinster tries it on, it only fits one foot – that of Cinderella.

Story:
A beautiful young woman impoverished by her father's death is forced to cook for, tidy and clean the household of her wicked stepmother and ugly stepsisters. When the palace announces a ball for its eligible prince, all the spinsters of the region are invited to attend but Cinderella is forbidden by her stepfamily. Miserable, she is left behind but a magical fairy godmother intervenes and conjures Cinderella a gown, glass slippers and coach to take her to the ball. She warns that Cinderella must leave before the stroke of midnight or her coach will return to a pumpkin, her gown to rags. Cinderella meets, dances and falls in love with Prince Charming but when she flees at the stroke of midnight, she loses a slipper. Bereft, the Prince hunts for the woman he wishes to marry by allowing

every spinster to try on the magical glass slipper that fits only one foot and even though her stepfamily do everything to prevent Cinderella from meeting the Prince, she is finally allowed to try on the slipper because they know it couldn't possibly belong to their poverty-stricken housekeeper. Cinderella becomes a princess.

Okay, now have a go at doing this for *Goldilocks and the Three Bears* or *Little Red Riding Hood*.

When you feel you've got a clear perspective on plot and story through this exercise, have a go at working out the themes, plot points and storyline for your own novel.

Give yourself up to ten main plot points and allow 500 words for your storyline.

THE BUSINESS END OF
BECOMING AN AUTHOR

SUBMISSIONS

Some of you are going to hunt down an agent and others may go direct to the publisher.

Keep in mind they are looking for the next new and terrific talent to present themselves to them, so they will welcome a well-targeted submission. But while your manuscript has likely consumed your thoughts, it is meaningless to an editor or agent at this stage so please don't expect them to be frothing at the mouth for it; they will get to it, they will read it and they will let you know.

Keep your obsession to yourself. Remember that these people in publishing are busy, busy, busy. They are all stretched thin: multi-tasking and looking after the authors they already have in their stable and are generating sales from. Then are they sifting through the towers of submissions from other hopefuls, of which you are only one.

If you would like to submit direct to the publisher, head online and read everything you can about that specific publisher. Make sure the company publishes your genre or you're wasting everyone's time.

Check the individual publisher's submission guidelines. Some companies might want hard copies, others might want the whole manuscript, while others will want only a couple of chapters. I suspect you'll find that all publishers these days accept digital submissions. However, give the publisher what it wants, exactly how it wants it.

Following is a useful guide.

Leader page

Include your name, contact details, the working title of the novel and a word count.

Manuscript

- Header: working title and your name, a telephone number is handy.
- Footer: pagination.
- Font: in the old days of paper submissions Courier New was the preferred font, which, although ugly, was easy on the eye. 12 pt. Today with digital submissions, I'd recommend you use Times New Roman or Georgia – note they are both serif fonts. Again, check the submissions guidelines for the individual publishers.

- Double-line spacing.
- No graphics or cutesy images.

Synopsis

You need a sparkling synopsis. Again in the old days of fifteen years ago, the synopsis could be more exacting, a bit flatter. However, our fast-moving world has changed this and I believe your synopsis should be snappier, used more as a sales tool.

Just as the blurb on the back cover might well be the first introduction a reader has to your novel, the synopsis is what the commissioning editor reads first, instantly making a judgement on it even if she doesn't intend to. She might think, does this sound like something I want to work on? Does my publishing company want it in its stable? Does it fit us? Is it interesting? Will it sell?

Limit your synopsis to around 400 words – don't exceed 500 words. No more than a page. I would urge half a page if you can. The snappier the better. Remember, you are not simply summarising the story arc but selling it.

I recommend that you work very hard on it to keep it punchy. Think about how well movies taglines can sell a movie. I'm not suggesting you need to present the synopsis in a series of one liners but it's instructive to start thinking in this succinct and crisp way about your novel. Know your work's theme and how to summarise that story arc under 500 words.

Practise making your synopsis shorter, sparer in its

presentation of information, more alluring in how it sells the story.

If you want other material to work with before plunging into your own, try writing the synopsis for some of your favourite novels.

REVIEWING YOUR MANUSCRIPT

Write it, *then* polish it!

Editors look at your work objectively and think about how a reader responds to it. They look first at the overall structure of your work, how it fits together as a whole; then they examine key areas like character and style; and then they look at details like spelling and punctuation.

The trick to self-editing your manuscript successfully is to try to think like an editor.

The most important first step in polishing is to actually not polish at all but to try to get some distance from your manuscript. This will help you find your own objective editorial eye. When you have finished your draft try to leave it alone for as long as you can. Ideally, leave it alone for a few months. When you take it out again and re-read it you will be looking at it with fresher eyes and far more objectivity.

Next, approach your work in a different frame of mind. It might help to think of yourself as an editor who is reading someone else's work. How do you react to it? You can't be author and editor at the same time. Leave behind your writing alter ego when you're ready to go back over your work with a critical eye. This will help free you from the demands of being the writer and allow you to see the work as a reader would.

Don't start re-writing your work at this point either. Keep in mind that an editor wouldn't rewrite your work, so nor should you at this point. Many writers read through their work and see a problem early on, in chapter three for example, and start fixing it immediately. Then they become tangled up in chapter three and, before they know it, they've taken off the editor's hat, put the writing hat back on and have lost the chance to get an objective sense of the work as a whole.

Read the manuscript through once, in its entirety, without stopping to fix anything, without even a pen in your hand. Just read for story power.

When you get to the end, jot down all the thoughts you had. This is how an editor reads a manuscript when they're doing a structural edit because it allows them to get an idea of the overall structure of the work without becoming distracted by the smaller details.

So, looking at the overall arc of your story:

- Does it have a satisfying beginning, conflict and lead character? What about the excitement and the initial drama being introduced?
- Are there any plot gaps?
- Is anything confusing?
- Are there unnecessary parts, such as a character or subplot?

- Are the characters working? Demanding that you follow their story?
- What about the overall voice and point of view?

Write down your first impressions and remember to include positives. It's very easy to be critical but it's important to focus on the things that you've done well. You can use these strong elements to then build on the areas that aren't working as well.

This is the big picture – the first layer of review – that will lay the foundation for the rest of your polishing. It may require some large-scale rewriting and if that's your decision, now's the time to move back into writing mode.

Once you have resolved the structural issues, you can move onto the next layer of polish. It's time to get a little closer to the text. Examine your dialogue and your characterisation, look at whether you are telling the reader things rather than showing them, look at your use of adjectives and adverbs, your balance of descriptive and active writing. Don't be afraid to cut words, characters or even whole scenes. Be brave and your work will be stronger as a result.

Now it's time to start looking at your work line by line and making sure it's as professional as possible. Most people think that fixing up typos and checking your grammar is what polishing means but this is the last part of a long process.

When you have been through all of these steps, then you will have a much more impressive and professional piece of work. Polishing requires a lot of patience and hard work, but your manuscript will be much stronger as a result.

Please go right ahead and congratulate yourself because finishing a manuscript is a great achievement, so have confidence in your abilities and be proud of what you have written.

THE INTANGIBLE ASPECTS OF BEING A SUCCESSFUL, PUBLISHED AUTHOR

Most people who are successful in their careers possess certain qualities that make it as easy as possible to do business with them. There are exceptions, of course, but in the main, the 'let me know and I'll fix it' attitude will help you in immeasurable ways.

I know my attitude makes a valuable contribution to why I am still making a living from writing books, and for that reason publishers are happy to hear from me and consider my next projects.

It is so much easier for the person holding the purse strings to say yes to a project – in any situation, not just the publishing industry – if it's a calm, easygoing, generally happy person that they are dealing with.

If *calm, easygoing, generally happy* is not your natural temperament, then it would be wise for you to be aware of your shortcomings as a public relations supremo and work hard to present yourself at least as 'user friendly' in your daily dealings as a writer, especially if your manuscript is picked up and you become a part of a publishing stable. Let's talk about some aspects to consider.

No one enjoys a needy author

It's exciting to be handed your first book contract. Other than being handed our twin sons for the first time, I'm not sure what else in my life has come close to that private joy. Publishers and agents know this, so they too enjoy your pleasure and are incredibly happy for you and perfectly understand your enthusiasm.

Be conscious that you don't instantly triple their workload by becoming a serial pest: emailing or phoning constantly for information on this and information on that, or worrying unnecessarily about the book's cover when you haven't even tackled the structural edit.

Finding your grace

We're not all happy-go-lucky personalities but to get on in this business don't make it difficult to be liked. The archetypal moody artist does not make for an easy journey as a commercial fiction writer. And humility is a wonderful thing, even now that you're seeing your book on shelves all over airports!

If you consider yourself just a tad too important to sit in a draughty space outside a bookshop in a shopping mall at a lonely signing table for an hour, where not a single book customer exchanges a word with you other than to ask you the way to the nearest toilets, then don't write commercial fiction. This is a scenario you could well face. I have – many times.

Commercial fiction writers will shoulder the main responsibility for marketing their books and that may well mean in-store signings where one or two people may stop for a chat but not buy a book. It may be that no one turns up. In times like these, the smile shouldn't waver and the thanks to the bookstore manager for stocking your books and helping you with a signing must be ready and genuine. Remember, they had to set up the table, buy in extra stock and make sure a member of staff was available; perhaps they even ran an ad in their local paper or radio station and then, out of embarrassment, when no one turned up, they let you sign twenty of their books that now must sell.

If the publicity team organises a radio appearance and it turns out to be local community radio in a grubby back-street and the proffered coffee mug looks only vaguely rinsed, treat it as though you're walking into the hottest radio station in the country and turn on the performance as though speaking to the masses. It is a valuable part of the learning curve to come across well on radio.

Or if you're asked to give a talk at a library and only five people turn up – one of whom has clearly come in from the cold and wants a nap – talk to these five people as though you're addressing five hundred adoring fans. It's a great way to practise your public speaking skills.

If someone comes along to one of your appearances at a bookstore just to stop you for twenty minutes to talk about the thriller they've been writing for the past six years, be interested and be encouraging, don't look bored and distracted. It isn't always about *you* simply because a publisher has bought your book. Never forget how it felt when you were waiting for your first manuscript to be acquired, when you'd have given anything for a published author to listen and maybe give you a few minutes of advice. Remember, this person taking your time is also your reader. They may have bought your book for which you are eternally grateful and if they haven't, maybe they will – especially because you were so gracious. What's more, they could well be plugged in to chat rooms, websites, blogs, forums, they may review books for online magazines or for booksellers. You just don't know. Do not give them the cold shoulder because they appear inconsequential now that you're a big-time author.

Graciousness is a truly admirable quality in anyone and it shines within writers for whom it comes naturally and draws people to them – it sells books too! Grace can be learned, of course, so be aware of your body language, your ready smile, your interest in others and, above all, your old-fashioned good manners. That latter one goes a long, long way.

I have sat at a signing desk where no one was queuing to buy my books but there was an almost comically long queue for the writer next to me. Tell yourself that every dog has his day, but if it's not to be this day, you must be gracious. Chat to the people waiting for their books to be signed by the other author, make them laugh and take the pressure off the other author who is signing but doesn't want to hurry the people whose books they are signing. You may be surprised how many people say, 'I'll buy one of yours next time.' Or, they may decide they like you enough that they buy your book on the spot. Whatever happens, the queue of people will remember you and talk about you, and the other author will thank you for helping to relieve the pressure.

I know this sounds hard to credit – perhaps you want to believe all books are bought on the merit of the story-telling – but my experience shows that it's not always a simple equation of strong storytelling. If people *like* you, because you're charming and interested in them – you've made them laugh or been interested in the baby in their arms – they *will* buy your book. They'll buy it even if they don't normally read your genre or they prefer not to buy a debut novel or they really don't have the money to do it.

This leads me to my next point, which is so important I'm going to put it under its own subheading...

Approachable, fun, inspiring authors sell books

Resist the desire to flex the claws. You are always going to hear about other writers and their *faaaaabulous* manu-scripts. If this occurs when you've just received a rejection of sorts – not necessarily of your manuscript but maybe the advance is less than you'd hoped, or the book is only coming out in B format, or the huge department chains

will not be carrying it, or it won't be in the Christmas cata-
logue, blah blah blah – then work hard not to show your
frustration by bitching. It has a horrible way of coming
back to bite you.

I have always had a rule not to talk about other writers
unless I love their work. If I hate their work – or even dislike them (hey, we're not all perfect) – I don't get drawn
into discussions about them or their books.

There is a fine line, of course, between saying you didn't
enjoy a book for this reason or that – it's perfectly accept-
able to have an opinion, for you are a reader like anyone
else and entitled to like or dislike. But don't get personal,
avoid gossiping. Don't savage another person's work – who
knows better than you how hard it is to fill so many blank
pages with a story? And there's an editor and a publishing
team somewhere that loves this book and there is likely a
host of readers who love it too. The fact that you don't love
it doesn't mean it shouldn't be treated respectfully, or risk
that sharp tongue/keyboard returning to haunt you.

We are in a small industry in Australia and everyone
knows everyone, everyone talks, and all the editors, agents,
publicity teams in each publishing house are all quite
friendly and stay in touch.

Don't you know who I am?

I know that this sounds stunningly obvious but it needs
to be said.

If you can't find your books in a bookshop, don't go all

purse-lipped on the staff and ask to speak to the manager. There are many reasons why it's not there, including that they didn't want to order it – yes, suck it up! – and no amount of debate will change the fact that the book is not there. And it will definitely not be there in the future if you make a scene.

More often than not it's just an ordering issue or warehousing problem and the book is likely on its way – perhaps it's in boxes out the back waiting to be unpacked.

If other writers you know have been invited to attend a literary festival or are being paid to give a talk at such-and-such place and you have not, don't start suffering deep angst. It happens. The reason people are chosen for events range dramatically. It may be that the theme of someone's story fits the theme of the festival or that the author bumped into the event organiser in a supermarket and one thing led to another. It's that luck and timing thing I've spoken about.

I'm arguably one of South Australia's happy success stories in commercial fiction and, fifteen years on, at the time of writing I am still waiting for the Adelaide Writers' Week to acknowledge I exist other than as an emergency filler. Nor has Melbourne, Sydney or Brisbane noticed me. I have never let it trouble me. One day I may be invited to speak at one of our major festivals and I shall graciously accept.

It can feel as though everyone around you is enjoying more 'success' than you: winning awards, gaining grants, being asked to attend events or give keynote speeches. Their book posters are plastered over bookshop windows and in airports, and they are featured in magazines. Stay calm! We all feel this at one time or another and it is likely that we're magnifying what we're seeing and blowing it out of proportion.

We all have to do our time in obscurity. It takes years to be noticed and even longer before you become that writer that bobs up in newspaper articles to make a comment or the author that magazines are happy to feature.

You know you're wonderful and have so much to say and you know your books are worthy, but you must be patient until the public catches up with you. If your books are popular and if you are affable, easy to approach and accessible, then a busy journo will eventually pick up the phone to call you because you make it simple for them to get a quick comment or to get a quick 250-word piece on whatever the topic it is that they're working on with a nasty deadline.

Serial Deadline Killer

Speaking of deadlines, do not become a serial deadline killer. One of your most important responsibilities as a commercial fiction writer – especially if you want to keep signing new contracts with higher advances – is to *make your deadlines*.

As a newly acquired novelist you may not yet have a grip on life in a publishing house. It's a steep learning curve and you will soon gain a healthy appreciation of just how thinly spread people are. One thing you can count on is that everyone is working to deadlines, from the acquisitions and contracts stage through to editorial, sales, marketing, publicity and warehousing: it goes on and on.

Yes, *your* book is very important but it is not the only book your editor is working on. And although there was all that hugging and smiling and congratulations six months previous, the fact that you are not the centre of your editor's world six months on does not mean you are not on her radar. You are. Be assured that when the magical deadline viciously rolls around for when you agreed to deliver your first draft, your editor will be looking for that manuscript to arrive. And suddenly you will be the centre of attention again. And you would want to ensure you're making her life as easy as possible by hitting that deadline.

I am one of those annoying goodie-two-shoes who invariably delivers before deadline. Seriously annoying to others, perhaps vaguely unnecessary for the editor but smug central for me. Early delivery means I can tick a very important box, and so can my editor: she knows it's there and waiting for her at her convenience. I don't think I know a single senior editor who would complain that her author is 'always delivering early'.

Deadlines are the beat that the whole publishing industry marches to, from authors at inception to booksellers at the coalface. Books have dozens of dates attached to them: delivery dates, structural edit dates, copyedit dates, proofing dates, galleys deadlines, cover art meeting dates and on it goes through to publication day.

If you as the originator of the work miss a deadline, you can see how it affects a long line of people who are depending on your timely delivery to keep the production and publication schedule for that one title on track. Now, I will say, there is always some fat in the editorial deadline but don't rely on it. In fact never rely on it.

Be the writer who surprises by delivering on the day you've been asked and I can assure you, you'll be a writer with a gold star by your name in the publishing house. Is this important? Hell, yes! For a start, which editor wouldn't want to work with a person so reliable? Authors who constantly run late on deadlines, who need their editorial team to keep begging for more time down the line, who in turn create headaches for others because they requiring 'special handling' make their editor look bad. At meetings she's the one who has the red face, who is making apologies and asking everyone else to please understand. Do that a couple of times and that editor is going to start making excuses for why she isn't keen to keep working with you.

Let's say we have two authors submitting new manuscripts in a similar genre – one is a romantic tale set in the 1960s and the other is a contemporary romantic novel. They've had a couple of books each with this publisher and, although they haven't been best sellers, they've done enough to prove that as writers they have potential and should be nurtured. The publishing house can only buy one new manuscript in this genre – they'd love both of course but it's too risky. Although lots of other aspects come into the equation, for hypothetical reasons let's say all is equal. Is it easier to buy the manuscript from the writer they know will deliver to deadline and be easy to work with, or will they buy the novel from the drama queen who has a track record of being flaky on deadlines? Hmm . . .

On Editing

It is during the editorial process that you will show your true colours to your publisher.

It is perhaps during the structural edit and copyedit that you will be at your most emotional. If you are attached to your manuscript in the way that I am attached to, say, our sons, then you are going to have your good humour challenged during editing. I do not love my manuscripts in a way that comes even close to how I love our boys, which means I handle editing well.

If you are in love with your words, you are going to have to dig deep and find the courage to let them go, because some of them *are* going.

I personally couldn't care a fig about what the editor suggests regarding my manuscript, providing I can understand the rationale. And if my editor is suggesting 25 000 words are to be pruned, I will usually shrug because I know I'm not being punished – in fact, the opposite is true.

The main point I want to make here is that you really do need to approach editing with a cheerful outlook. It's absolutely no good hating the notion that someone is hacking into your work and then showing that loathing by being disinclined towards change or constructive criticism.

Remember, if you make it easy to work alongside you, contracts will flow.

And be confident in the knowledge that your editor is *on your side*!

Touring

You know you've made it when your publisher wants to tour you. This may change as authors become increasingly accessible online through Skype, through blogs, via their websites, Facebook and Twitter.

But as I write this, my publisher is planning the next book tour. For the time being touring remains one of the main marketing weapons in the publisher's arsenal for getting a writer out and about among their readers.

If you are offered a tour, take a breath and understand what is behind this.

It's not a jolly. It's not a bonus. It's not even the publisher saying well done. You are being toured because the publisher can make money out of you but in order to make that money the marketing team is going to spend a lot of money in the following ways, some of which often get lost in the mind of the authors:

• A publicist will probably travel with you full-time.

- You will be transported in cabs and limos, rarely required to heave your fragile body around on its own legs.
- You will be put up in nice accommodation – if not in high quality hotels, then in quality apartments.
- You will be wined and dined for the entirety of your time away from home.
- Your publicist will be seeing to most of your needs, for example fetching you a water before you go on stage, getting you on time to all functions, adjusting a schedule if you've run overtime and so on.
- You will fly on fares that are interchangeable, so you'll get good seats.
- You may even be taken into airport lounges.
- You won't actually have to think for yourself for the time you're away.

Do not abuse this. Your publicist is a hardworking, highly intelligent person who is not there to peel you a grape at 3 a.m. or to carry your luggage. She is there to ensure that you get to where you are meant to be on time, stress free as best as she can organise and in a happy frame of mind. Let's not forget this same person has worked very hard and creatively to organise media for you, just as she has bolted together the events schedule. Don't complain, don't sigh, don't gasp to the heavens when a bookseller suddenly changes schedule on you. Laugh, go book shopping, take a coffee break, check email, do some work. You're a professional writer now. Be professional. Be a strict time-keeper, dress smartly for all public presentations, thank your hosts. You are never too tired, never cranky.

PAY IT FORWARD

Do:

- Encourage other writers wherever you can.
- Share your success and don't be precious about your time, work and commitments.
- Give advice generously if someone asks for it.
- Recommend other people's fiction, not just your own.
- Buy books: keep the money circulating in the publishing industry.
- Host a book club: the fact that you're published adds weight to the gathering.
- Support your local library if they ask for it, and give your time gladly.
- Support the community where you can. It's lovely to have value placed on your time but don't insist on payment for everything. Some communities simply can't afford to pay you but need your support.
- Use your author status on social media to help promote the festivals and events of local communities and libraries.
- Join your local writers' centre.
- Join the Australian Society of Authors. It's your

lobby group in parliament. It is our public advocate and needs our financial support.

- Attend festivals and literary events: support these projects.
- Pass on manuscripts to your agent and/or publisher if they are worthy.
- Spread good news stories from the literary community.
- Congratulate other writers: be excited for them.

At the time of writing this I have hosted four master-classes with just over seventy writers passing through its doors. Another two are in motion in the coming three months with fifty people involved. I am in touch with all of them – I make myself available to them via my private email, through Facebook and face-to-face at various events. I invite those who have succeeded with a commercial publisher to return to the masterclasses so they can speak about their experiences and give their advice and hints. I am invested in their ongoing careers and help wherever practicable, usually through one-on-one advice. I am never too busy for a masterclasser, never short of some encour-aging words. I take this attitude because the masterclass is one of the main ways that, in a hectic schedule, I am able to sit still for long enough to plug into the community of new writers. I make sure I am not only focused on them through the week but that I am available to them weeks, months and years later, when no funds are exchanged. It is all about helping a fellow writer, caring about emerging talent and knowing that often it's the right words from the right person at the right time that can make all the difference.

A few don'ts:

- Don't denigrate the writing achievements of others. If you've got nothing good to say, don't say anything. (This is different to genuinely critiquing a novel. You are a reader and you are permitted not to enjoy a story and say so with a helpful explanation why you didn't enjoy the reading experience.)
- Don't encourage others to troll for you in cyberspace. Earn your good reviews through your solid storytelling.
- Don't get wound up by what other writers are achieving. Every dog has its day, remember? Bide your time and be patient.
- Don't *ever* accept a pirated copy of someone else's work.
- I personally believe it is poor manners to use another author's social media pages to spruik your own book, for instance, 'Oh yes, that's a valid point, Fiona, I did just that with my book called *Blah Blah* that is coming out next month with Blah, and please LIKE my page'. Bear in mind that the author whose page this is has worked hard to get

her profile to where it is, her publisher has no doubt invested lots of marketing dollars too, so respect that you need to tread your own path and not stand on the shoulders of others – not without being invited to do so.

THE FINAL CHAPTER

So, how are you feeling now that you're at this point?

I'm hopeful that if writing a novel previously daunted you, you now feel more assured. We're sharing stories; don't blow it up into something bigger. Storytelling should be fun, not stressful. Write because you love it.

Here's a summary of how I feel about writing commercial fiction.

A novel comes together through the discipline of many writing sessions so it's wise to stop viewing it as a *huge* mountain in your life. Don't dramatise it to the point where you don't want to face it, or to the point that you risk boring those around you because of it. The way to approach it is to see it as small inclines that you ascend frequently. Don't look down (back through the manuscript) and don't look up (and frighten yourself with the amount of story you are yet to cover).

I take the attitude that the only words that matter are today's words. Yesterday's are written. Tomorrow's are coming. Stay in the moment and focus on today's word count. When those words are in the vault, ruthlessly walk away from your keyboard and get on with your life. That's the discipline I live by and, I promise you, a book will shape itself around that routine if you make it yours. Don't speed, don't slow down – it's about a steady clip to the finish.

Never lose sight of the fact that your job is to entertain in your storytelling. If your novel isn't engaging, then a publisher will not acquire it. It's not their fault they don't love it. It's your job to make it irresistible.

Mainstream commercial fiction is not always about what you want to write and what you think everyone should read – no one cares, remember, until you make them care. Instead, commercial fiction is entirely about what people want to read. The fact that you've always wanted to write about a lobster called Larry is great – write it just for you but don't get miffed when you face a pile of rejections and then blame the publishers. Blame yourself instead.

Money, money, money should be ker-chinging in your mind because that's what makes this circus go on tour. If everyone involved can make money from your story, then you have something commercial to go ahead with.

Do that homework. See where you fit in, where your

style of writing fits, where your story ideas work best and for whom. Who is your audience? Which publisher takes on manuscripts like yours? Are the stories that you want to write selling now? If they're not, then you're probably writing for yourself. There's nothing wrong with that but if you want to write what people want to read, then go and discover what's selling and from there, decide whether you can write it.

Be philosophical – it might well turn out that you re-alise you're not cut out for commercial fiction and you're deliciously happy writing stories that please you – and perhaps family and friends – and that you're prepared to enjoy the journey of self-publishing so that you can share those stories at your own pace. I say, terrific, because you've worked it out.

Writing is a lonely business. Be very sure about this. And while you're lost in the world and events of your novel, the people closest to you, especially your partner, are potentially going to feel deserted. Email my husband to learn more! But we got this sorted out at the beginning and, as I've mentioned, I'm very disciplined so I'm always around to cook for and enjoy time with the family. That said, Ian and I have definitely lost some special 'our time' together because my work is so isolating. As I put our boys ahead of anything, they would probably shrug and say they've never been aware of missing out on me but I know Ian, who was used to us working side by side in our previous business, does feel the withdrawal that writing a book prompts. He's wise and patient enough to know it's not personal and, most importantly, that I will make time for him when my day's writing is done.

Talk to the special person in your life to be certain that you both go into this writing adventure open-eyed, and so that you know that you've been honest and have their support. And then you must promise yourself to make an effort to give special time to your partner. Ian and I research together. Heaven knows I need his eyes and ears and focus – he sees so much and takes in so much that I miss. However, the time travelling is time we get alone, and when we're not researching together we spend time talking, laughing, reading, sharing. Make that time, whether it's for a breakfast every Sunday morning with just the two of you or going to the movies every Thursday evening. Have some designated time that your partner can count on, which has nothing to do with other family needs and is not about the writing. You'll thank me for this. It's crucial for healthy, happy relationships. Do not let the writing consume you. It's really not that important!

For those who desperately want to write commercial fiction and join the horde of competitive novelists out there, strap on your armour, harden up, get disciplined and get going. No more excuses! And stop caring so much about how important this is to you, because, hard truth, no one else is interested.

Some tips to leave you on:

- Turn the television off. Limit your social media interaction. Stop looking at your phone (it makes you look needy). Read instead.

- Share with your friends and family that you are writing and that you must have time alone to do that but be fair about the time you give to your writing. Family responsibilities come first.

- Don't be repetitive. Don't be repetitive. It's annoying.

- Don't be dull. You need conflict! Drama! Tension!

- Flowery sentences and blousy overwriting will get you slammed. I love Stephen King's take on this, who asks, why use long sentences when you can use short? It's not a shameful thing. He shows it so well when he compares this pretentiousness to dressing up a household pet in evening clothes. As he says, both the pet and the owner are embarrassed, because it's completely excessive. I'm laughing just picturing this again!

- And on the topic of language, hunt down and destroy every cliché, all those adverbs, most of those adjectives and indeed conjunctions that can be, for the most part, substituted by a full stop. Remember: simple, pared-back language is best for commercial fiction. Think of your story as an exquisite little black dress – let it do the work, don't adorn it too much.

- Each conversation and each scene in your story must be relevant. Just because you travelled to the North Pole to research your book doesn't mean it deserves its place in your story because unless there's a point, unless there's a clue in the scene to the story, unless it has a subtext, it might as well be a travel column.

- Accept that what you write cannot please everyone. Also accept that you won't write as smoothly now as you'll be writing in a few years' time, once you have lots of practice behind you.

- Go deep with your storytelling. Takes risks. Confront the hard stuff – it makes compelling reading.

- Character is plot. Whatever your characters are up to is what makes the story move. Focus on everything your characters are doing; that's what makes people read on, not your marvellous descriptions. Keep those descriptions rich, succinct and authentic so you can evoke a keen sense of place.

- Winning an emotional response from your reader is your key responsibility – that and making sure the pages turn themselves. Both of these elements will ensure that the pleasing ker-ching sound keeps ringing.

I wish you confidence because that's what undermines so many new writers. Believe in *you*, believe in your storytelling and know that it's going to get better the more you write. People never have and never will never tire of stories. There's a hungry audience out there – now, go get 'em!

... ...

REFERENCES

COMMERCIAL FICTION PUBLISHERS

Research a publisher that specialises in your chosen genre and then check online for their submission guidelines. There are now more opportunities than ever to pitch unsolicited manuscripts direct to publishers. Alternatively, research appropriate literary agents via your relevant writers' centre (details below).

The major publishers have different imprints under which they release their authors' works. Each imprint has a different identity and is connected to a book's genre and reader demographic. For instance, when I was writing fantasy, I was released under the Voyager imprint at HarperCollins. Voyager has a dedicated editorial and publicity team that specialises in speculative fiction. At Penguin Books – the home for my commercial fiction of the romantic adventure kind – I am published under the Michael Joseph imprint, which has a vast reach into the general women's fiction market. Penguin has a range of imprints that cater to a variety of writers and audiences: from Destiny, its e-first romance imprint, to Hamish Hamilton, which publishes literary fiction and nonfiction.

Allen & Unwin

allenandunwin.com/default.aspx?page=462

Hachette

hachette.com.au/Information/ManuscriptSubmission.page

HarperCollins Publishers Australia

wednesdaypost.com.au

Pan Macmillan

panmacmillan.com.au/manuscript_monday.asp

Penguin Books

penguin.com.au/getting-published

Random House Books Australia

randomhouse.com.au/about/manuscripts.aspx

Scribe

scribepublications.com.au/about-us/manuscript-submissions

WRITERS' CENTRES

One of the most important things you can do for your writing career is to seek support. Connect with other writers and stay abreast of key events by joining your local writers' center and the Australian Society of Authors.

Australian Society of Authors

asauthors.org

1800 257 121

ACT Writers' Centre

actwriters.org.au

NSW Writers' Centre

nswwc.org.au

NT Writers' Centre Inc

ntwriters.com.au

Queensland Writers' Centre

qwc.asn.au

South Australian Writers' Centre

sawriters.on.net

Tasmanian Writers' Centre

tasmanianwriters.org

Writers Victoria

writersvictoria.org.au

Writing WA

writingwa.org

PUBLISHED RESOURCES

There are lots of helpful books to turn to that can help you with construction of sentences and understanding grammar. Here are a couple of examples:

How to Write Better English: Penguin Writers' Guides
    Robert Allen

Style Manual: for authors, editors and printers
    Revised by Snooks & Co

ACKNOWLEDGEMENTS

Bryce Courtenay stepped into my life on three occasions and each time shifted my perspective and pathway. The first time we met, in the year 2000, he convinced me to write commercial fiction and so began an exciting journey. In 2009 he insisted I was ready to tackle writing mainstream fiction; I made the leap and not once have I regretted it. In 2012, when he was desperately ill, he asked me to continue his legacy of helping aspiring writers to believe in themselves. He handed the baton to me for his Commercial Fiction Masterclass and, as reluctant as I was at the time, I couldn't deny him. I took the baton and soon discovered the honour he had bestowed. The privilege of guiding others has enriched my life, my work and my writing.

So, thank you to all the brave Masterclass alumni, who

have made it through boot camp and my terrible dancing – seeing your confidence and commitment explode through our week together makes me proud. Those who have made that big jump from wannabes to novelists brandishing commercial publishing contracts or have pushed on into self-publication – you thrill me and remind me that the hard work of Masterclass is always worth the investment. And here's to those yet to pass through the week where epiphanies occur and writers learn to believe in themselves and their storytelling.

I subscribe to the notion that when the student is ready, the teacher arrives – as Bryce arrived for me. There is no doubt I've had plenty of help along the way from other writers who have inspired, notably Robin Hobb, who came along at just the right time. Not enough can be said for having nurturing publishers and I've been lucky, especially with Stephanie Smith and Sue Brockhoff in Australia and a fine host of publishers internationally. In the Penguin family, Robert Sessions in the early days and later Ali Watts and Ben Ball, your triangle of influence has been huge since 2008. Thank you to Clementine Edwards who helped me to edit this work and heartfelt thanks to all the Penguins in my life: brilliant to work with, always open to my ideas.

Behind any writer is usually a host of family and friends. My cheering squad is robust and loud, most notably my trio of Ian, Will and Jack McIntosh; draft readers, in particular Pip Klimentou; and, more recently, Nathan Giaccio who has been a cornerstone for Masterclass. Love and thanks to my crew.

While I take the business of writing novels for my publisher seriously, storytelling for me is fun, creative, escapist as it should be for any commercial author. I think I'm one of the luckiest people on the planet to write books for a living and to have such a wonderfully generous audience including the marvellous booksellers that we should all hug. Keep writing and/or buying books, everyone.

THE LAST DANCE

*Would you risk
everything for love?*

Stella Myles is suddenly impoverished through a family crisis and becomes forced to make ends meet by selling herself as a dance partner in a Piccadilly ballroom. Here she meets the enigmatic Montgomery, who orchestrates a job for her as governess for the wealthy Ainsworth family in Sussex. But nothing is as straightforward as it first seems.

In entering the mansion of Harp's End, Stella encounters a family with more secrets than most. She struggles to fit in above or below stairs – although nothing proves so challenging as restraining the illicit love that ignites between herself and the mysterious Douglas Ainsworth.

When Douglas announces that they are all to voyage aboard a cruise ship bound for Morocco, tensions reach new heights and finally bubble over. Stella finds herself caught up in a family at war and in a world on the edge of another. She is now the keeper of an incendiary document smuggled out of Berlin, one which must reach London at all costs.

**From the rolling green hills of the Kentish Weald
to the colourful alleys and bazaars of Morocco,
this is a thrilling story of intrigue and danger –
and a passion to risk dying for.**

NIGHTINGALE

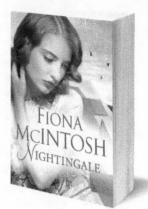

A breathtaking novel of heartbreak and heroism, love and longing by a powerhouse Australian storyteller.

Amidst the carnage of Gallipoli, British nurse Claire Nightingale meets Australian Light Horseman Jamie Wren. Despite all odds, they fall deeply in love. Their flame burns bright and carries them through their darkest hours, even when war tears them apart.

When Jamie encounters Turkish soldier Açar Shahin on the bloodstained battlefield, the men forge an unforgettable bond. Their chance meeting also leaves a precious clue to Jamie's whereabouts for Claire to follow.

Come peacetime, Claire's desperate search to find Jamie takes her all the way to Istanbul, and deep into the heart of Açar's family, where she attracts the unexpected attention of a charismatic and brooding scholar.

In the name of forgiveness, cultures come together, enemies embrace and forbidden passions ignite – but by the nail-biting conclusion, who will be left standing to capture Nurse Nightingale's heart?

**Love comes out of nowhere
for most of us, when we least expect it.**

'Fiona McIntosh is a superior writer in the genre, and if you enjoy popular romantic fiction, you'd be mad not to try her.'

THE AGE